Beyond Brokenness

Louis A. Smith and Joseph R. Barndt

Friendship Press · New York

Editorial Offices: 475 Riverside Drive, New York, NY 10027
Distribution Offices: P. O. Box 37844, Cincinnati, OH 45237

Contents

A Word to Our Readers

Doing mission requires first both hearing and listening and then responding. The very format of this book is designed with both hearing and responding in mind. Starting on page two each left-hand page throughout the book presents the author point of view or story. Starting on page three each right-hand page throughout the book offers the reader the opportunity to respond either to the left-hand pages or to the illustrative material on the right-hand pages. Where questions are raised on right-hand pages you may want to discuss them in a study group or respond to them individually. Where space is provided on right-hand pages you may wish to write in your responses or thoughts. We suggest you first read straight through the left-hand pages and then re-read the book using the right-hand pages.

Part One

God's Mission

Part I

A. THE WORLD BENEATH OUR FEET

This book is a Bible study, but it does not start with the Bible. The subject of the study is our mission within the church, but that isn't where we are going to begin, either. Rather, the starting place for this study of the Bible and mission is the ground on which we walk, the reality of our daily existence. The entire first section, nearly one-fourth of this book, will be devoted to a description of the world.

The reason for such a point of departure is a strong conviction that God encounters us earthlings nowhere else but here on earth, in the midst of our earthly experiences. Not on some other worldly stage, but here among our shacks and suburbs and skyscrapers, amidst our dust and diamonds, the struggle takes place between God and Satan, between good and evil, between justice and injustice, between life and death. We begin this study by describing the reality of our lives because that is the arena in which the Bible describes God taking action, and because that is the environment in which we are directed to discover God's presence among us. Therefore, that is the setting in which the rest of this study will explore the mission in which God invites us to participate.

Even more important is the *reason* God breaks into our world and enters into our lives. Contrary to popular belief, God's mission is not to help us escape from it all. God's goal, rather, is to re-marry us to the world, to build a new relationship between us and the creation, a relationship that will last as long as we live. Of course, the Kingdom of Heaven and eternal life are ultimate goals, but they are already beginning to happen here and now with a new life in relation to God and to each other on earth while blood is still flowing through our veins and while we are still trying to figure out who should be the next president. God does not take us away from the world in order to save us, but in the midst of the world seeks to transform us, to change us along with the rest of the creation. The promise of the end of the world and the Kingdom of Heaven is not a rejection of creation but our assurance of its completion and fulfillment. It is not God's plan of redemption to turn us against the world as an enemy, but to call us back into the world as lovers who wish to serve it.

These assertions are by no means agreed upon by everyone. There are many, perhaps even among the readers of this study, who would strongly disagree. There are more than a few popular religious movements, some purporting to be Christian and using a Christian vocabulary, that are teaching exactly the opposite beliefs. They teach that God encounters us in purely spiritual realms unaffected by the physical and socio-political realities of our earthly lives. They teach that it is God's objective not to lead us into, but away from an essentially evil and undesirable world. Teachers of such doctrines find many willing believers in every stratum of our society. For example, people who are rich and successful might find a religion that provides a separation between divine obedience and worldly behavior to be a welcome addition to their already comfortable lives. On the other hand, for people whose lives are filled with suffering and loneliness, an escape into the purely spiritual and promises of total release when this life comes to an end, can be an extremely tempting and popular religion.

Such mixed feelings about the world as these are not unusual. They are as old and as common as the Old Testament writers' changing moods. On a bright cloudless day, the psalmist praises God for all the world and for everything that is within it. Yet, on other days, torn and agonized by the suffering and brokenness of the world, the preacher in Ecclesiastes wished he had never been born. This pulling in two directions is also a familiar experience for the disciples of Jesus. For example, the apostle Peter, dazzled by the pure, problem-freeing, power-giving light of the Transfiguration, began to design in his mind a

2

STARTING POINTS. What is your experience? Where is the starting place for a person seeking to do the will of God? What have been the major landmarks on the roadmap which has led you this far to an understanding of God's mission?

Do you look first at the world with your own eyes, and experience it with your own hands and feet? And then do you get some help in interpreting what you have seen and felt? Or, before you experience it for yourself, do you first learn from others what to look out for, and what it all might mean?

Does theory come before practice, or practice before theory? Do we think our way into new kinds of action, or do we act our way into new kinds of thinking?

Probably it is neither all one or the other. Many people, however, especially those who advocate a "theology of liberation," claim that we have had too much theory in the church and not enough practice. We need to do more experiencing and acting in the real world before developing our theology and our theory. These theologians give this action/reflection the name of "praxis."

". . .all of us are aware that doing theology is important; but it is a secondary thing in the Christian life. . .The first act, which is the act of liberation and of faith [must be] reflected when we start to do theology." (Gustavo Gutierrez, *Theology In The Americas,* ed. by Torres and Eagleson, Orbis Press, Maryknoll N.Y. 1976)

Everybody's favorite Bible verse, John 3:16, does *not* read: "God so loved the *church*. . .", or "God so loved *portions of the world*. . ."; rather it reads: "God so loved the *world*, that he gave his only son. . ."

Throughout this study the most important questions about mission will be directly related to your beliefs, feelings and attitudes about the world.

What does it mean to love the world?

Can we love God and the world at the same time?

Compare and contrast: John 3:16, John 17:14-18.

mountaintop monastic retreat center. But Jesus took Peter by the hand and led him down from the purified atmosphere, back to the city, the noise, the pollution, the conflict, down to the hostile hill by the garbage dump called Golgotha.

In the world or out of the world? This very same tension between a spiritual and a worldly understanding of Christianity can be found in our own lives. All of us have mixed feelings about the world in which God has placed us. Sometimes we want to compliment God on a job well done. Sometimes we wonder if an incredible mistake hasn't been made. Longings toward heaven and tuggings toward earth—which way do we feel called?

On the other hand, perhaps the most important question is not about our feelings, but about God's feeling toward the creation, and about God's present activities within the creation and ultimate plans for it. The authors of this study have a strong bias that God calls us back into the world, calls us back to join in a mission of loving, caring and suffering with people while God goes about the long range task of making the creation complete and whole again. While openly sharing this bias on our part, we invite readers to struggle with this question, and especially with their own internal tensions which this question produces during the rest of the study.

The World-As-It-Is

In these next pages we invite readers to participate in an effort to describe the world in which we live, as seen through the eyes of its inhabitants. This will be a more or less "secular" or "humanistic" view of the world, without bringing a particularly Christian interpretation to what we see.

If this portrayal is to be accurate, our primary importance is the aim of being truly global in our view. We will attempt to reach beyond the experiences of white, middle class, United States Christians, emphasizing especially the Third World continents of Africa, Asia and Latin America. Of course, our own North American experiences are an important part of the whole, but they are still only a small part. The United States, for example, represents little more than six percent of the world's population.

THE SPIRITUALIZATION OF CHRISTIANITY

What kind of experiences have you had with religious teachings that relegate God and goodness to the purely spiritual? Perhaps one of the most familiar groups with such an emphasis is the religion called *Christian Science*.

At the same time, almost every Christian denomination has been affected by dualism. As early as in the writings of St. Paul, the confrontation can be seen between the Hebrew's unified view of the world, and the dualism of the Greeks. Although the language of Christianity has been strongly influenced by dualism, and although many people believe that dualism is Christian, the teachings of Christianity strongly affirm a wholistic view of human beings and of all creation.

Is it possible for two expressions of feelings about the world to be more contrasting than the following?

Print out the words of Psalm 148:5-12 here:

Print out the words of Ecclesiastes 4:1-4 here:

Our own life's histories can produce contrasts equally as strong as these. If you have ever kept a journal or a diary, read back over it, and note your ups and downs, the variations of your moods. Make some notes here.

Recall and collect a list of cotemporary writings, films, events, etc. from your own experience and that of others, which portray this contrast of optimism and depression about the world, or rapture and despair.

Seeing ourselves within this much larger context may seem a little strange to us at first. We are more accustomed to being the world's main feature. All else is usually interpreted in terms of the strength and power and technological achievements of the United States and the predominantly white western world. As can be seen in the accompanying map, this ethno-centric view of the world has even influenced and distorted our physical pictures of the world.

As we attempt to picture our world in its global proportions, we will also include descriptions of both our individual and our corporate existence. In both of these dimensions we will examine first the condition of brokenness and suffering, and the return over the same paths to search for signs of joy and wholeness.

If we are able to achieve a consciousness of our worldly reality, we will be better able to ask the second question of this study: where and how does Scripture teach us that God enters into and acts within this reality? And then, the third and final question, which takes up the last half of this book: how does the Bible describe the possibilities of our joining God and sharing in this mission in the world?

Signs of Brokenness in the World

It is difficult to look at our brokenness. We usually avoid it as long as we can. We put on masks to cover up our problems. When we can, we look at the world through rose colored glasses, pretending that nothing is wrong. But beneath the masks and the glitter, there is a sick and suffering world, and within it are the majority of the world's people who cannot afford the price of the masks or the pretense. Let us have the courage to look at ourselves without the masks. Let us try to look at ourselves and the world as they truly are. For it is only by facing this brokenness that we can prepare for the gift of being made whole again.

Personal Brokenness: Climb on board life's treadmill. Scramble for the platform of success. Become number one. Grab hold of your bootstraps and pull yourself to the top of the

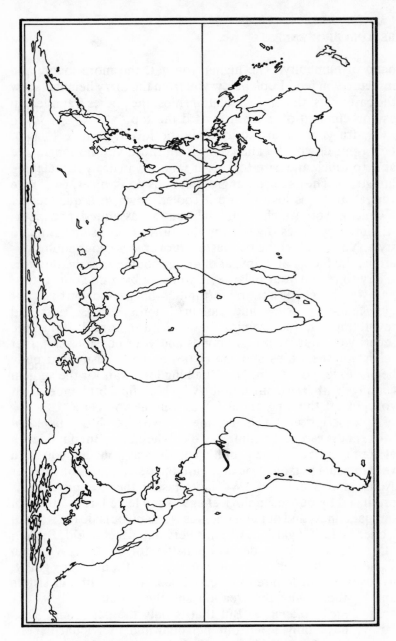

Why the strange map of the world?
[Comparative size of continents]

Approximately 400 years ago Mercator created a map to help European sailors on their voyages of discovery. It was to become the definitive world map. His cartographic representation is a distortion. It is European-centered and helped determine the way people have looked at the world. The new map (above) by Arno Peters shows the equator at the center, and gives an accurate presentation of the land size of different continents.

heap of humanity. The higher you get, the more lonely and insecure you feel. Look below you from the dizzy heights. View the casualties, the broken relationships, the bodies trampled on as you climbed over them toward the top.

Mourn your failure to love and be loved, your feelings of being put down, the alienation from those you no longer are able to touch and care for. Your family watches you watching life go by. They see you angry that ends don't meet, your rage where once was love before it cooled down to acquiescence. Helpless, you watch your children be assaulted and over-whelmed by drugs, by sex, by the glitter of consumerism and style. You still feel the bad taste left over from your adulterous affair, the feeble attempts at marriage counseling, the divorce.

Try to regain your balance as you stumble into your forties, past your prime, past the opportunities that passed you by. Your new fears are crime and violence in the streets, riots and revolutions in the evening news. You're afraid about the security of your stocks and bonds and your pension plan. Get ready for the fifties and the sixties as your mistreated body begins to let you down. Now the long long wait for the sudden coming death, the confrontation with life's final brokenness that you put off thinking about for as long as you can.

A description, such as the above, of life's personal brokenness can be repelling and overwhelming. But if it doesn't at least in part describe your life and the way you feel, you are a very unusual person. You and I are the descendants of Brother Adam and Sister Eve. We have tasted the deceptive fruits produced by our technological age. They have left us aware of our nakedness and our aloneness as we stand outside the walls of a once beautiful garden, within a very imperfect world. Broken in spirit, we wage a desperate battle for control. We train ourselves to be more aggressive, to say no without feeling guilty, to cover up our failure to love and be at peace with our sisters and brothers, with the creation and the Creator.

Systemic Brokenness: But that is only the beginning. Thus far we have only listed our personal and individual experiences of brokenness. Even longer and more frightening is the picture of brokenness that can be seen in society's corporate systems and structures. With impersonal efficiency they arrange

Can you love with me yet this universe, its energies, its
   secrets,
its earth still good,
its air, still unmasked at least,
its fire, sign of night's hope,
its water, quenching, even inexpensive?
Dare we hope to love each other yet?
(*James Carroll, Elements of Hope,* Paulist Press,
   Paramus, 1971)

The three main areas this study will explore:
1. The World, a place of brokenness and a place of struggling
and yearning to return to wholeness.

2. The World, the focus of God's mission to bring healing and
wholeness.

3. The World, where we receive the benefits of God's mission,
and where we receive the call to join God in this mission.

Return to this page after reading through this study and
re-define these three areas as you now understand them.

Your own personal sense of brokenness: Explore, in terms of
your own experience, the validity of the sketch of human
brokenness in the opposite column. Check it out against the
history of your life and that of your close friends.
Use a separate sheet to write a parallel history of your own.
How is it different? How is it the same?

Many people in our society insist that each individual is
responsible for having chosen the positive and negative directions
in his/her life. Others look more to societal and cultural causes of
success, failure, etc. What do you believe?

9

and maintain suffering and brokenness on a mass basis.

Once upon a time, justice could be easily measured by the presence or absence of integrity in individual actions. These separate acts had limited effects upon a few persons at a time. Now justice or injustice is done by massive and complex systems with simultaneous effects upon tens of thousands and millions. Now the most significant measurement of brokenness is the way in which the many are helplessly exploited for the benefit of the few. Our lives are increasingly determined by uncontrollable economic systems, transnational corporations with greater power than most nations, computer systems that store and recall information while satellites flash it around the world at the will of those who own them.

For profit and for power we are divided and pitted against each other according to our sex, our class, our race and our nation. Our otherwise relatively harmless personal prejudices, hates and fears are harnessed together to create maximum destructive force. Worse, still, we are deluded into willful cooperation. We are led into believing the awful lie that the slaughter of millions by warring nations within this century alone was necessary, was for our own good and was the will of God. We are systematically programmed to believe that the continued manufacture and maintenance of incredibly destructive weapons is not suicidally and criminally insane. We are conditioned to repress into semi-consciousness the corruption, waste, pollution, and the failure of systems which were originally designed to provide law, justice and order. As a people we are standing at the pinnacle of success and the precipice of catastrophe. We are the children of parents whose sin is being visited upon our generation. And we are afraid.

Oppression On A Global Scale: A very small percentage of the world's people—predominantly from white and western nations—have attained the power to consume and expand at will, making use of the natural resources and human labor of the rest of the world to achieve their goals. Those others in the rest of the world—the vast majority of the population—live in poverty and powerlessness. They are the "culture of the oppressed" who barely have the food, shelter, clothing and

A PARABLE OF GOOD WORKS

Once upon a time there was a small village on the edge of a river. The people there were good and the life in the village was good. One day a villager noticed a baby floating down the river. The villager quickly jumped into the river and swam out to save the baby from drowning.

The next day this same villager was walking along the river bank and noticed two babies in the river. He called for help, and both babies were rescued from the swift waters. And the following day four babies were seen caught in the turbulent current. And then eight, then more, and still more.

The villagers organized themselves quickly, setting up watch towers and training teams of swimmers who could resist the swift waters and rescue babies. Rescue squads were soon working 24 hours a day. And each day the number of helpless babies floating down the river increased.

The villagers organized themselves efficiently. The rescue squads were now snatching many children each day. Groups were trained to give mouth-to-mouth resuscitation. Others prepared formula and provided clothing for the chilled babies. Many, particularly elderly women, were involved in making clothing and knitting blankets. Still others provided foster homes and placement.

While not all the babies, now very numerous, could be saved, the villagers felt they were doing well to save as many as they could each day. Indeed, the village priest blessed them in their good work. And life in the village continued on that basis.

One day, however, someone raised the question. "But where are all these babies coming from? Who is throwing them into the river? Why? Let's organize a team to go upstream and see who's doing it." The seeming logic of the elders countered: "And if we go upstream, who will operate the rescue operations? We need every concerned person here!"

"But don't you see," cried the one lone voice, "If we find out who is throwing them in, we can stop the problem and no babies will drown. By going upstream we can eliminate the cause of the problem."

"It is too risky."

And do the numbers of babies in the river increase daily. Those saved increase, but those who drown increase even more.

—from "The Fifth Commisson"
newsletter, vol. V., no. 4.

health necessary for survival. And even more significant than their poverty as a sign of brokenness is their powerlessness to challenge the dictatorships which control them, and to change the structural reality of their conditions.

We have seen these people, the "wretched of the earth" who so out-number us. In this age of mass and instant communication, with cameras and microphones scanning the earth for daily news, they seem to be before our eyes at every moment. We try to respond to the reality of their hunger with programs of aid, of development, of international loans, of charity. Yet nothing seems to change. The emaciated body and distended stomach of the child with her hand held out toward us pleadingly, does not go away when we turn the page.

All such responses made by "developed" nations to the needs of "underdeveloped" nations are based on the belief that the conditions which brought about our richness can be duplicated. Our hope has been that our formula for success can be copied, and it is only a matter of time and energy before global development begins to take place.

The opposite belief, however, is held by vast numbers of people throughout the world. They believe that there is a causal relationship between the conditions of our richness and the condition of global oppression. The single most important, as well as the single most volatile, question being debated at this moment of history is the extent to which our wealth in superabundance is dependent upon poverty and powerlessness in others. It is a question of whether our economic system is the potential cure or the principal cause of the rich-poor divisions in the world.

This question raises much defensiveness in us, of course. It goes against the grain of much of our national ideology, our national identity, and our national religion. But it is on the basis of this question—more than any other question—that decisions are being made and battles are being fought, decisions and battles that will determine for many years to come the lines between brokenness and wholeness in our world.

The Final Brokenness: So it goes, a macabre dance of brokenness, that we are unable to stop, until we reach the final brokenness. Then it does stop of course. Death comes. Ready or not, with the sudden fierceness of the ultimate sign of our

It is obvious that the world cannot afford the USA. Nor can it afford Western Europe or Japan. In fact we might come to the conclusion that the earth cannot afford the 'Modern World'. It requires too much and accomplishes too little. It is too uneconomic. Think of it: one American drawing on resources that would sustain 50 Indians! The earth cannot afford, say 15% of its inhabitants—the rich who are using all the marvelous achievements of science and technology—to indulge in a crude, materialistic way of life which ravages the earth. The poor don't do much damage; the modest people don't do much damage. Virtually all the damage is done by, say 15%. It is obvious, therefore, that the Club of Rome exercise, which lumps all people together into a 'world population' and also lumps all production and all consumption together, as if everything were much of a muchness, far from clarifying the tense situation, obscures it. The problem passengers on Space-ship Earth are the first-class passengers and no one else.

It is hard for us to believe that the rest of the world sees us as their oppressor. If it is true, we are not conscious of it. Read the following quote about unconscious assent to being oppressors. Do you agree?

"The philosophy of oppression, perfected and refined through civilizations as a true culture of injustice, does not achieve its greatest triumph when its propagandists knowingly inculcate it; rather the triumph is achieved when this philosophy has become so deeply rooted in the spirits of the oppressors themselves and their ideologues that they are not even aware of their guilt. . . .Injustice is more a work of the social machinery, of the system of civilization and culture, than it is of people's intentions." (Jose Miranda, *Marx and the Bible*, Orbis Books, Maryknoll, N.Y. 1974)

brokenness, we all come to this life's end, and the earth is poured back over us. A few saints, like Francis of Assisi, can calmly call forward an invitation to "brother death"; but most of us live in stark fear of its coming. We are a death-denying people who pretend to be caught by surprise every time a heart stops beating.

The fact of death and of our inability to face it affect us far more profoundly than a long forgotten appointment that suddenly comes due. Our wisest philosophers and teachers point out that our fear of living and our failures at loving are directly related to our fear of dying and our failure to accept our death. For many, whose lives are lived in constant tragedy and despair, physical death is only a confirmation of that which happened to their minds and spirits long before.

This present age of systems and technology has affected the fact of death, like it has affected everything else. For some people, this effect has been a positive one: the visit of the grim reaper has been deferred for a little while. With the advancement of the medical arts, one can plan on a longer and fuller life; death can be put off for as much as a decade or two.

But for a greater, even incalculable number, technology has affected death in the opposite way. Death has been systematized, made into a horror far greater than all the Dantes and Hitchcocks can portray. Six million Jews exterminated in the Holocaust. Three million dead in the United States war on Vietnam. Uncounted millions killed in warfare in the twentieth century. Our skill in helping people to die is far more advanced than that of helping them to live.

But whether or not assisted by technology, it is inevitable that death comes for us all. While our young bodies are growing and gaining strength, we feel eternal. We have no time or need to think of death. Then, as our bodies begin to weaken and deteriorate, as we begin to wonder about a life beyond this one—whether we have done enough good to deserve it—we become more and more afraid of this ultimate sign of our brokenness. Then when death does come, it finds most of us only able to say, with surprise, "So soon? Why it seems like I only just got here!"

14

And thou most kind
  and gentle death,
Waiting to hush our
  latest breath,
O Praise Him, Alleluia!
Thou leadest home
  the child of God,
and Christ our Lord
  the way hath trod.
O Praise Him, Alleluia!

St. Francis 1182-1226

The Serpent: Did God really say you were not to eat. . .?
. . .No! You will not die!

Genesis 3:3

That is why we despair; that is why we would welcome
The nursery bogey or the winecellar ghost, why even
The violent howling of winter and war has become
Like a juke-box tune that we dare not stop. We are afraid
Of pain but more afraid of silence; for no nightmare
Of hostile objects could be as terrible as this Void.
This is the Abomination. This is the wrath of God.

We who must die demand a miracle.
How could the Eternal do a temporal act,
The Infinite become a finite fact?
Nothing can save us that is possible:
We who must die demand a miracle.

Signs of Wholeness and Joy in the World

Alongside the brokenness and suffering is the other dimension of life's reality: the experience of wholeness and joy. In its fullness it is usually described as existing only in memories of times past or in visions of achievements yet to come. But for nearly all of us the experience of wholeness and joy comes at least partially to the present time, a welcome visitor alongside the sometimes bitter struggles of life. This section's task is to search out signs of life that reflect this perspective, to attempt to describe that part of our reality which still remains unbroken, or which once broken is now healing and becoming whole again. Our goal in this section, as in the previous section dealing with brokenness, is to provide a realistic setting within which in the rest of our study to grapple with the questions of God's mission and activity in our midst.

It is of critical importance that our description of wholeness and joy not exist independently of the previous discussion of brokenness and suffering. A dualistic view of the world would have us view these two aspects of life in total separateness of one another. It would describe the experience of beauty and pleasure as independent relief valves, temporary escapes which help us to be better able to re-enter the true world which is an unchanging world of evil.

A more wholistic understanding of reality will picture these two aspects interdependently. The experience of physical illness, for example, displaces a condition of health and creates in us a yearning and a striving toward becoming well again. So also in every other aspect of life, the experience of brokenness recalls to us the memory of unbrokenness and a vision of the possibility of completeness. The connecting points between our condition of brokenness and wholeness is the human struggle to overcome forces of evil and to be free human beings.

Thus, the beginnings of an answer to the question, "Where do we look for signs of wholeness and joy?" are rooted in the question itself. The beginning of wholeness is in the human desire and struggle for it to exist as an alternative to brokenness.

The United States Constitution states that the "pursuit of happiness" is a basic right of all humans. It does not say,

Getting There Is Half The Fun

How do you describe a full, complete and happy life? Usually it is talked about in the future tense. Each of us has a vision and a hope for the day when everything is going to be all right.

But the experience of this other side of life does not depend on its complete achievement. We sample parts of it every day of our life. What's more, it is the experience of most people that the greatest joy in life comes from being in the struggle for a better society, and not just from reaching our final goals. The experience of the "good life" comes when in the midst of our brokenness, we join together with others to care for each other, and to overcome the cause of our pain.

What do you think?

All the political goodwill and all the instruments of social and economic development at the disposal of the rich and poor countries must be combined and be harnessed with a new spirit of dedication, sacrifice, wisdom, and foresight to meet our common obligation to the whole of humanity. This calls for a new and global vision of man and the human race. . . . The challenge is not just simply the elimination of poverty, ignorance, and disease. It is first and foremost a question of building a world in which every man, woman, and child, without distinction, will have and exercise the right to live a full human life worthy of his or her person, free from servitude, oppression, and exploitation imposed on him or her by other fellow human beings; a world in which freedom, peace, and security will have practical meaning to each and every member of the human race.

> Kenneth Kaunda, President of Zambia, at the Fourth Assembly of the World Council of Churches, Uppsala, Sweden

however, whether it is right that some people catch up with it, and others do not. Nor does such a constitutional provision relate to the experience of most of us that the surest guarantee of happiness slipping through our fingers is to make it the central goal of our grasping. Nevertheless, while we cannot evade the issue of unequal distribution, we can at least begin by looking at some of the joyful aspects of life that are common to all, such as the sights and smells of Spring, the touch of one you love, music's rhythms, the taste of food and drink, the strength of human community and companionship. These and a thousand other pleasing experiences are neither isolated nor accidental. They are the results of the unceasing productivity of nature, of continuing human creativity, and of the persistent search for human community.

In nature, seeds fall, they die, new life springs forth. Food is produced and eaten. Even its waste and leftovers are used by nature as nutrients for new lives, as well as in the eons-long process of manufacturing fossil fuel, diamonds and the like. From the universe's explosive beginnings to this very moment's heartbeat, nature's productive and recuperative powers are the roots of our existence upon which we are fed and sustained.

Nurtured thus by nature and given life, we invent, construct and organize, leaving behind us the marks of human creativity. Our singing, sculpting and painting, our poetry and classics, our playing symphonies and games of sport—are all beauty marks of our humanity. Above all, the end goal for which we search and strive, for which nature and human creativity are our tools, is the achievement of human community.

Howevermuch we are constrained by hostility and competitiveness, our desire for wholeness and joy leads us into personal relationships of love and trust; it calls us into vocations and professions of human serving; it gives us the courage to risk our resources, our individuality, our lives for the sake of others. In life together, in small and large communities, sometimes strong and sometimes fragile, always yearning to be strengthened and reproduced, can be found the strongest and most abiding sign of human wholeness and joy.

Striving For Systemic Wholeness: The most powerful witness to this human longing for wholeness in our day can be seen on

18

Consciously or unconsciously, much of what we do is based on an optimistic view of the future. Can you add to the following list?

Getting married
Having children
Getting up in the morning
Planting a seed
Starting a revolution
Going to a doctor
Going to church
Forming a committee
Passing a petition
Asking questions
Protesting injustice
Telling the truth
Saying, I love you

We live in a new world of exciting prospects. For the first time in history men can see the unity of mankind as a reality. For the first time in history we know that all men could enjoy the prosperity that has hitherto been enjoyed by a few. The new technological possibilities turn what were dreams into realities. The adventure of cooperation with all men for the development of the earth for all men is open for all of us, and youth at least is aware of its pull. As today we have the means, so we are without the excuse of ignorance about the condition of men throughout the earth. It is one world and the gross inequalities between the peoples of different nations and different continents are as inexcusable as the gross inequalities within nations.

Report of the Beirut Conference on World Development, sponsored by the World Council of Churches and the Pontifical Commission on Justice and Peace, p. 16

systemic, institutional levels. This should not be at all surprising. If our portrayal of increasing systemic oppression in previous pages is accurate, then it is also on this level that we should expect to discover creative resistance to brokenness. In our nation and culture we are being confronted with a number of systems in which our people have for centuries been able to place their confidence, but which are becoming less and less adequate for our needs. It is in the midst of the breakdown of these systems that the oneness of the human family feels most threatened. Therefore, efforts to develop and build new systems that encourage and sustain community and systemic justice are the most treasured indications of new life today.

In the context of these strivings against systemic oppression and yearning for more adequate systems, there are at least three clear signs of wholeness and joy. The first of these is the *survival of the oppressed* in the face of the greatest of odds. As we have already noted, conditions of suffering and oppression are the normal state of life for entire nations and peoples. These conditions have continued for long periods of time, often with little hope of their ever being resolved. Despite immeasurable suffering, death and seeming hopelessness, such people exhibit an incredible endurance and an ability to survive. Among such people has evolved a "culture of the oppressed" that can scarcely be understood from without. That which is passed on from one generation to the next within these cultures of the oppressed is not only the determination to survive, but also a strong love of life and vision of freedom.

The second of these hopeful signs is that oppressed peoples not only have the power to survive, but also to strongly resist their oppression. Since the beginning of recorded history, wherever there has been systematic persecution and tyrannizing of a people, there has been, along with the ability to survive, an accompanying indestructible resistance of oppression and struggle for liberation. In the contemporary global situation, this can be seen as the experience in nearly every country in Latin America over the past thirty years; it has been likewise the case especially in southern Africa, in Vietnam and in many other countries in Asia, as well as among oppressed minorities of the United States.

Read the words of some famous leaders of movements to resist systemic injustice.

"If a man happens to be 36 years old, as I happen to be, and some great truth stands before the door of his life, some great opportunity to stand up for that which is right and that which is just, and he refuses to stand up because he wants to live a little longer and he is afraid his home will get bombed, or he is afraid that he will get shot. . .he may go on and live until he's 80, and the cessation of breathing in his life is merely the belated announcement of an earlier death of the spirit.

"Man dies when he refuses to stand up for that which is right. A man dies when he refuses to take a stand for that which is true. So we are going to stand up right here. . . .letting the world know we are determined to be free."

Martin Luther King, Jr.

"But we two—Baptist Pastor and Catholic Bishop, US and Brazilian citizens—are not discouraged. There is hope, and there is a great dream of a world in which there will be no more misery, no more war, no more prejudice, and all men will be free. This was the dream of Jesus Christ, of Mahatma Gandhi, and of Martin Luther King, Jr. This is our dream, too."

Ralph Abernathy and Dom
Helder Camara, The Declaration
of Recife, March 1970

"At the risk of seeming ridiculous, let me say that the true revolutionary is guided by a great feeling of love. It is impossible to think of a genuine revolutionary lacking this quality. Perhaps it is one of the great dramas of the leader that he must combine a passionate spirit with a cold intelligence and make painful decisions without contracting a muscle. Our vanguard revolutionaries must idealize this love of the people, the most sacred cause, and make it one and indivisible. They cannot descend, with small doses of daily affection, to the level where ordinary men put their love into practice."

Che Guevara, 1965

The cruelest and most ruthless dictators in the world always seem surprised and dismayed to discover this unquenchable revolutionary spirit among the people they seek to keep in captivity. Those who place high values upon freedom, justice and self-determination, however, see in these efforts cause for joy and celebration, despite the great costs in human pain and suffering that are exacted from those who participate in such struggles.

The third of these signs of hope can be seen in efforts to create alternate systems. Struggles to eliminate systemic brokenness call for the creation of new systems that are more whole and just. Beyond the ability to endure and survive, beyond the assurance that the oppressed will inevitably rise and rebel, there is the need to believe in the possibility of alternate systems of government and economics, of production and distribution of resources, of education and communication.

In our world and in our day it is possible to observe, study and celebrate various attempts of people and nations to create such alternatives. Decolonized nations such as Nigeria, Jamaica and Angola struggle to create situations where their development will serve the needs of their people. In nations such as Tanzania, Cuba and China, there are experiments with various forms of socialism. In China, for example, new systems of production and distribution are making it possible to provide food, clothing, health and shelter for nearly one billion people—one fourth of the world's population! In the United States, there are innumerable experiments in alternate systems of food production, energy production, education, etc. Behind each of these many efforts is a yearning toward the future, a hope in the creative capabilities of humanity, and a vision of the possibility of wholeness and joy that can overcome the brokenness and suffering which often seem to dominate our world's everyday reality.

The Real World and the World of the Bible

In the first part of this study we have been attempting to develop a sketch of the "real world" in which we live. Our thesis

22

Yearning for new life and resisting oppression may look quite different in our own middle class oriented society. Wholeness and joy for us—and not only for the poor and oppressed—has something to do with our refusing to consume so much, being willing to give up our overabundance of power and wealth.

Look around you. Where do you see people seeking happiness and new life in this way? What kind of movements or organizations have you taken part in that have goals to resist in these ways?

The Alternative Lifestyle

There are hundreds of experiments taking place in the United States, to create alternative systems. They include alternative schools, housing and energy, alternative police systems, alternative communities and communal living, alternative diets and drinks; and the list goes on.

Some of these alternative experiments have been more successful than others. Some last for long periods of time; some die very quickly. What has been your experience?

has been that this "real world" or Monday through Saturday, and not a purified Sunday morning version, is the world in which God promises to enter and act, and in which God calls us to serve. The rest of our study will attempt to describe this mission of God's and ours in the context of this "real world" that we have been describing.

Before moving on to this central theme, there is one aspect of this thesis that is possible for us to test in advance. Our statement that God enters into our world and acts within it, is based on the assumption that the world we have been describing corresponds to the world that is described in the Bible. Our final concluding task in this section is to confirm that there are indeed parallels between the "real world" in which we live and the world of the Bible.

Our tendency is to think of the Biblical world as being more spiritual than the secular orientation we have when we watch the ten o'clock news. In fact, when the Biblical writers looked at their world and described the situations in which they experienced God acting, their descriptions of brokenness, suffering and need were quite comparable to our contemporary situations.

For example, if you re-read the descriptions of the world and its wickedness in which Noah lived before the flood, you will be clearly put in mind of the wickedness we have been describing here of our own world. Or if you read again the description of Sodom and Gomorrah before their destruction, you will undoubtedly begin to think about our urban centers, many of which could be quite comparably described. The image of the Tower of Babel could also be applied to any number of present day idolatrous situations which have the clear objective of outdoing the work and power of God.

Listen further to the Old Testament writer's record of alternating feasts and famines which drove the people of Israel into their fateful relationship with the government of Egypt. Picture the experiences of Israel's oppressions in Egypt before the Exodus, and compare them to a description which a modern Israeli would give as justification for their latter day military conflicts with a twentieth century Egyptian government.

The broken world of the Bible, into which God enters and

24

Do you hae difficulty thinking of the Bible stories taking place in a flesh and blood world such as ours?

Does Cecil B. DeMille's idea of the Bible's world cause you to do "mental gymnastics" on Sunday morning?

Have you ever heard someone say, "The teachings of Christianity just don't work in the real world"? What does such a statement mean?

acts, is a world quite comparable to the situation in which we live today. The people whom the angry prophets addressed as unjust and oppressive, the conditions of which the mother of Jesus sang and of which Jesus spoke, and even the explosively apocalyptic images of the Revelation; although such matters as styles of clothing and sophistication of communication are quite different, the primary reality of brokenness is the same.

There is a similar set of parallels in the pictures drawn by the Biblical writers of the struggles for wholeness and joy in their experiences of the world. They saw broken people in a broken world, searching and yearning for the words that would give their personal stories a happy ending. They saw communities, whole peoples and nations striving for the directions that would bring them to justice and rightness. They discovered signs of wholeness and joy among those great heroic individuals such as Abraham, Isaac and Jacob, Rachel, Ruth and Rebecca. And they held up thousands of others, less well-known seldom-named people as illustrations of the human strength to overcome the obstacles of life.

Likewise, they saw in the nation of Israel a special example of a people's ability to survive oppression under the tyrant's heel in Egypt, in Babylon's exile, and in their own land while under the rule of the Roman invader. Not at all unlike the irrepressible yearning for freedom that we earlier described in Latin America, the Biblical people of Israel also could not be contained for long by her oppressors. Again and again its overpowering enemies learned that Israel not only refused to die, but also refused to remain silently and passively imprisoned. And finally, in the nation of Israel, the Biblical writers found an example of a people willing to commit themselves to the design and construction of a new society dedicated to the principles of justice and rightness.

The Biblical writers describe their situation in terms of interweaving signs of brokenness and wholeness, in order to demonstrate both the needs for and evidence of divine intervention into an otherwise hopeless situation. Onto the stage of human brokenness comes the Creator with a mission to make the world completely whole again. The yearning and struggles of the people for new life demonstrates to the Bible's

Use this space to print in two sets of Scriptural passages from the Old Testament describing the "broken world." Try using two translations of the Bible. Clues for where in the Bible to look? See left page.

readers not only that God is at work accomplishing this task but also that he calls his people into this task with him. It is to examine this part of the story, both in the world of the Bible and in our own real world, that we now move.

Use this space to print in two sets of Scriptural passages from the New Testament that speak to the concept of community. Try using two translations of the Bible. Clues for where in the Bible to look? Try the books of John and Acts.

B. GOD
THE ACTOR

Introduction

We now turn to the central tasks of this study: to discern the Biblical understanding of Christian mission; and to use this understanding to explore the question of Christian mission in the world we live in today.

The use of the word "actor" in the title of this section is intended to suggest the image of a stage play. As the idea of Christian mission is popularly understood, it is we who are the chief actors. The spotlight is on us and on our responsibility as Christians. While we are the chief actors, God is a combination script writer, director and prompter. He is the one who lays out the mission and whispers our lines, but we are on the stage. The play usually begins with our asking, with dramatic and exceptional fervor, that familiar question about mission: "What does God want me to do?" Then the play continues with us as the chief actors, seeking answers to the question, and designing programs and activities to put the answers into action.

Our definition of mission in this study has God coming out from behind the scenery and acting on front stage center. The spotlight is not on us, but on God. God has always been and still is now the chief actor. The central question of the play is not, "What does God want me to do?", but, "What is God doing?"

Mission, from the Biblical point of view, is God's mission. We are called to join God and participate in that mission. As we shall see later in our study, our participation is of two kinds: first, to receive and benefit from God's mission; and second, to

Here are some excerpts from a church mission statement of the 1960's. It was considered radical enough to cause strife within the church which adopted it. Can you think of why that might have been so? Compare these statements with your own congregation's statement of purpose.

"We affirm in faith, humility and joy that the mission is the Lord's; He is the great doer and sender.

We affirm that the mission is not an optional activity in the church, but that the church is caught up in the manifold and dynamic mission of God.

We affirm that the church is God's mission.

We affirm that the church is Christ's mission to the whole world. . . .

We affirm that the church is Christ's mission to the church. . . .

We affirm that the church is Christ's mission to the whole society. . . .

We affirm that the church is God's mission to the whole person and will minister to the needs of the whole person, not because we have forgotten the witness of the Gospel, but because we have remembered it."

31

join with God in mission in the world. Our main task at the moment, however, is to emphasize that it is God's mission, that God is the chief actor.

At this point we should say something of how we intend to use the Bible in this and succeeding sections. Most everyone who reflects on the subject of mission places the Bible in the center of those reflections. We do that also. But our main intention is to use the Bible as an aid in discerning the *current* mission of God. Therefore, we want to allow the Bible to engage our contemporary world—the world we attempted to describe in the previous section. It is our hope and confidence that allowing the Bible and our contemporary world to interact freely with each other will be of help to us in discerning the mission of God.

To continue one step further with the image of a stage play. The Biblical stories can be seen as "flashbacks" to earlier acts of God, while simultaneously the play continues in the present with God still the chief actor. While our main focus is on the question of what God is doing *now,* the study of the Bible as a "flashback" helps us to understand how and why God is acting as he is today.

God's Mission Is Creation

The first thing that can be said about God's mission from a Biblical point of view is that it is a mission of creation. Also, the last thing that can be said about God's mission is the same: that God is the Creator. It may sound strange at first, to put it this way, but all that God does can be listed under the heading of creation. As the chief actor in mission, God creates. It is inaccurate to locate creation way back at the beginning of the Bible, and then to describe the rest of God's work as something totally different—called "salvation". God's total mission, from beginning to end, is creation; even the work of salvation serves that mission of creation.

According to some people you might get the idea that God's original plan changed somewhere along the line. According to some people you might think that God is no longer about that creative activity, but is now trying to get a small fragment of our

The Creed

"I believe in God the Father Almighty Maker of heaven and earth. What does this mean?

"I believe that God has made me and all creatures; that he has given me my body and soul, eyes, ears, and all my limbs, my reason, and all my senses, and still preserves them; in addition thereto, clothing and shoes, meat and drink, house and homestead, wife and children, fields, cattle, and all my goods; that He provides me richly and daily with all that I need to support this body and life, protects me from all danger, and guards me and preserves me from all evil; and all this out of pure, fatherly, divine goodness and mercy, without any merit or worthiness in me; for all which I owe it to Him to thank, praise, serve, and obey Him.

"This is most certainly true."

Martin Luther, *Small Catechism*

What do you think of the following Bible Camp ditty?
"Heaven is a wonderful place
full of beauty and grace
I'm a gonna see my saviour's face
'Cause heaven is a wonderful place.
I wanna go there."

How does it compare with these words from a contemporary Christian writer:

"In any sanctuaries. . .where the preaching and teaching is about a fancied 'afterlife' instead of this life; about some indefinite 'hereafter' instead of the here and now; about immortality (which is actually an elaborate synonym for memory) instead of resurrection (which means living in emancipation from the power of death); about 'heaven'—as if that name designates a destination in outer space—instead of participation in a moral estate or condition; or about 'eternal life' as a negation of this life instead of the temporal fulfillment of life: where these or similar doctrines prevail, there is patent distortion of what the author of Hebrews calls 'the elementary doctrines of Christ.'"

(Hebrews 6:1-2). From William Stringfellow. *An Ethic for Christians and Other Aliens in a Strange Land.* p. 43

humanness (usually called our "souls") off the earth and into heaven. This is the activity that the word "salvation" is usually applied to, but it really seems a lot more like escape. God is pictured as trying to fix it so at least some part of some people escapes from this world.

The Biblical concept of salvation is something very different from this. God does save, no doubt about it! But *what* God saves is not only us, much less only a part of us. God saves the creation! Salvation is not a new idea on God's part, as if it were necessary to move from creation into something newer and better. Salvation describes God's work to restore the world to its state as perfect creation, and to restore people into their state of complete human beings. Salvation restores us to the kind of human beings needed for the world to be creation rather than chaos, whole rather than broken, just rather than unjust, alive rather than dead.

That which we know as the "story of salvation" is the story of God's mission to give us our humanness once again, to re-create God's image among us so that the creation can have what it needs: genuine, authentic human beings.

By creation, then, we do not simply mean the act of God's making "stuff". We mean the establishing and upholding of a world that might be described as "living together in love". Creation is God's total mission to earth; it includes all that is meant by such traditional concepts and symbols as salvation and justification, spirit-giving and sanctification, judgment and the fulfillment of the kingdom. God's mission of creation includes the entering of Jesus into our world of brokenness, into this world where wholeness is both a distant memory and a yearning and striving toward the future. God the actor enters into this world to re-create a marriage, to remarry us to each other, to the creation and to the Creator.

God the Actor: Making and Sustaining Life

Let us go to the beginning. If God's mission is creation, then it should be no surprise that the first mission statement in the Bible is the very first statement in the Bible: "In the beginning

Romans 8:19-23

"For the creation waits with eager longing for the revealing of the sons of God; for the creation was subjected to futility, not of its own will but by the will of him who subjected it in hope; because the creation itself will be set free from its bondage to decay and obtain the glorious liberty of the children of God. We know that the whole creation has been groaning in travail together until now; and not only the creation, but we ourselves, who have the first fruits of the Spirit, groan inwardly as we wait for adoption as sons, the redemption of our bodies."

Colossians 1:15-22

"He is the image of the invisible God, the first-born of all creation; for in him all things were created, in heaven and on earth, visible and invisible, whether thrones or dominions or principalities or authorities—things were created through him and for him. He is before all things, and in him all things hold together. He is the head of the body, the church; he is the beginning, the first-born from the dead, that in everything he might be preeminent. For in him all the fullness of God was pleased to dwell, and through him to reconcile to himself all things, whether on earth or in heaven, making peace by the blood of his cross.

"And you, who once were estranged and hostile in mind, doing evil deeds, he has now reconciled in his body of flesh by his death, in order to present you holy and blameless and irreproachable before him, . . ."

God created. . ." As the opening chapters in the Bible unfold, this fundamental mission of God is laid bare. God is creating a life-filled world all of which participates in "life together in love", or we might say, in community. God's goal in creation is a world in which God freely gives life and in which human beings receive it and share it with equal freedom.

In this creation human beings—male and female—are created in the image and likeness of God. What God gives to us so that we might be like God is our humanity. Since it is from the first a human community (and not just an individual) which bears God's image, we might better say that what God gives us so that we might be like God is our co-humanity.

Without a doubt human beings are not God: they do not have life within themselves. They are not self sustaining but are dependent on the gifts of God, especially on the other parts of God's creation, for nourishment. But these not-God creatures are nevertheless *like* God; so like God that one Biblical writer cannot conceal excitement over the prospect of being human:

"you have made *them* little less than God, and
crown *them* with glory and honor. (Psalm 8:5)

Not only is our humanity our closest connection with God; our humanity is also what the rest of creation needs in order for it to come to life. This often unrecognized item is made clear in both the first and the second chapters of Genesis. In the first chapter human beings are given a very special command: "be fruitful and multiply, fill the earth and subdue it and exercise dominion".

Under the onslaught of the destruction of the natural environment by human exploitation, this piece of the Bible's testimony has been seriously distorted, often by people of sincere and profound faith. "Subdue the earth and exercise dominion. . ." is not a license to misuse the earth! The text is a command to care for the earth! The command relates to our being in God's image, and the Genesis story makes it clear what that means. The image of God is not a domineering tyrant. The image of God is not an exploiting economic consumer seeking to absorb as much of the world as possible, like an eternal sponge.

36

Here is an alternative translation of Genesis 1:28
"Be fruitful and *be mature*; *fulfill* the earth and subdue it. *And exercise* dominion . . . . "

Compare this with the more common version: "Be fruitful and *multiply* and *fill* the earth and subdue it. And *have* dominion. . . ." What differences do you sense between the two?

A NEW HYMN ABOUT CREATION

Father creating a world of the present.
You still bring to being things that
　　were not seen.
Creating yet through us while often our
　　worship
Still glories in only what our hands convene.
Changeless Creator, Change Bringer and Maker,
You share your rule with us,
Your reign is willed through us
　　And call us to faithfulness to our own age.
Deluged by people, a world over burdened,
Where each new birth adds to the measure of stress,
Still draw us together in manifold places
Where knowing each other we care for the rest.
Present among us, yet shaping our future,
Transform us as people
New vision to carry
Yet known for our faithfulness to our own age.

The image of God is rather one who is a life-giver, one who shares and who creates others in order to have them participate in the sharing. The command to be fruitful and multiply, to fill the earth, subdue and exercise dominion over it, is not a set of permissive instructions to do whatever we please with God's creation. It is rather an opportunity to relate to the world in the same way that God relates to it: creatively, sharingly, life-givingly.

In the second chapter of Genesis, the story of ADAM (properly speaking "humankind"; the word is a collective noun, not the proper name of a male person) gives a similar picture. There we see the world languishing as a desert until the human being receives the breath of life from God and is raised up to make the desert into a garden.

Two things need to be said. First, Christian faith affirms that the God we know in Jesus Christ, the God who sends the Spirit upon all flesh, is none other than this community creating, garden planting God of Genesis. Second, the Christian faith affirms that the world described in Section I of this study—a world that is broken yet yearning for wholeness, filled with injustice yet pulsing towards liberation, alienated yet straining toward fulfillment—is the world which God intends to be "The Creation", and in which God would transform deserts into gardens that are cared for by his human creatures.

It is because God continues to create, to care for and to sustain the world that it remains a world of life and hope. The grass continues to grow, sometimes needing to force its way through cracks in the concrete. The land produces food, giving yet another opportunity for the human family to eat together in justice. Resources never imagined expose themselves to faithful human searchers. The world we call nature shows itself again and again to be God's creation.

We might sum up this first picture of God's mission in this way: God seeks to create a world which will be the embodiment of God's own life. In the course of doing this, God creates human beings, the kind of creatures who not only receive life but also share life and so enliven the rest of the creation. What the creator gives to us human beings so that we might be like God is our humanity. It is cause for wonder, but no cause for

We need to understand that it is in both the world of "nature" and the world of "society" that God continues to create.

Can you cite examples in each of those arenas which are signs of God's creative activity?

surprise that our humanness breaks through its own brokenness to seek for wholeness, for we have been created in the image of the ever-creating one.

God The Actor: Setting People Free

The story of the Exodus has been a primary example down through the ages of God's mission. Israel's deliverance from bondage is not only an historical event that proved to be a turning point in the restoration of the creation. It is also a paradigm, a model for restoration in our own historical situation.

Christian understanding of the brokenness that we experience in our lives has two dimensions. The first dimension of this "Fall of humanity" is expressed in terms of sinfulness and rebellion. The remedy for sin is forgiveness and the repentance which is included in being forgiven. The second dimension of our brokenness is explained in terms of imprisonment or enslavement, a condition of helplessness which requires rescue or liberation by an outside force.

Both of these dimensions are seen in the Exodus story. The sinful rebelliousness of the people of Israel (and even to a greater extent of the people of Pharaoh) is seen in their resistance and mistrustfulness of Moses. It is expressed most clearly in the post-Exodus period of wilderness wandering.

However, the condition of imprisonment is clearly described in the Exodus story as the most important cause of the Israeli people's situation of brokenness. It might even be said that their sin is rooted in their acceptance of their slavery. Healing and wholeness come as rescue, as liberation. What's more, liberation is not an individual event; nor is it merely the experience of an interior salvation. God's mission is to bring complete wholeness to the people and this includes leading them in a struggle for political/economic liberation that could be described as truly revolutionary.

It is no wonder that the Exodus story speaks so clearly to the situation of the majority of the world's people today, since they are also in situations quite comparable to the Hebrew people in

Read Exodus 1:1-15:21 asking:
Who is the major actor? What is the role of the Hebrews? What is
the role of Pharaoh? What is the role of the Egyptians?

The liberation of Israel is a political action. It is the breaking
away from a situation of despoliation and misery and the
beginning of the construction of a just and fraternal society. It is
the suppression of disorder and the creation of a new order.

Gustavo Gutierrez—*A Theology
of Liberation*

Egypt. And it is no wonder that liberation theologians find the Exodus story as a crucial starting point for reflecting on God's contemporary mission to restore the creation. Let us turn to a closer look at the Exodus story.

Even the most superficial reading of the story will reveal that it is God who is the chief actor in the Exodus. God hears, God comes down to deliver. God sends Moses and Aaron, causes the plagues, divides the sea. So much is God seen as the chief actor, that even the resistance of Pharaoh is attributed to God; it is God who hardens Pharaoh's heart! That kind of action on God's part may make most of us moderns a little squeamish. Would we dare say that the white regimes of southern Africa and the military dictatorships of Latin America resist the liberation of their people by God's design, so that when liberation comes they may take no credit for it? Does God really play the game that way? Would not God rather have reform within the repressive systems? Would we dare to say that the nations of the white western world will not release their strangle hold on the Third World nations because God is setting them up to knock them down? That is not our common way of talking about God, but it is the way things are told within the Exodus story. We should at least struggle with that language even if we can't come up with the final answer.

God's liberating action always takes place through some kind of instrument of his choosing. There are Hebrew midwives, Pharaoh's daughter and burning bushes; there are locusts and frogs. Sometimes it is a Hebrew slave; sometimes it is one of the oppressors. Always, there is the cooperating power of the natural world.

The most prominent instruments of God's action in the Exodus, however, are a preacher and a collection of environmental catastrophes: Moses and an assortment of plagues. Moses is the preacher of liberation for the Hebrew slaves. He preaches liberation to both the slaves and to their masters. Neither seem much inclined at first to respond with enthusiasm.

The response of Pharaoh makes it clear that the God of liberation is not recognized as God in the halls of power: "Who is the Lord that I should heed his voice and let Israel go?" Every

Go back to the first pages of this book and re-read with the Exodus story in mind. Can you think of modern happenings that reflect what happened in the Exodus? Here is a list of modern phenomena which have had the word liberation used with respect to them. In light of the Exodus story, in how many do you see God's liberating work?

Gay Liberation
Native American Movement
Black-Hispanic Struggles
Aged people
Handicapped and Mentally retarded children
PLO
Chilean People
Puerto Rican Liberation
Filipino Peoples

Can you add to the list? How many do you support? Take part in? Oppose? How do you go about defending or denying them as God's activity?

The Holy Roman Empire no longer exists, but there still remain in the Church many titles and insignia, many elements of ceremony and so forth of her visible aspect, borrowed at some time from the dazzling imperial splendor. Surely it is high time, and surely it would be to everyone's advantage, "to shake off the dust of Empire that has gathered since Constantine's day on the throne of St. Peter." These words were spoken by John XXIII.

once in a while, under pressure of a plague the Pharaoh appears to make concessions. But it lasts only until the pressure subsides and then he returns to his original position. There is never any structural change to which the Pharaoh agrees.

Such a story has been told many times down through history. Under pressure a wage increase may be won, but it is soon taken away by a price increase. Political concessions are soon worn away. Aid given to another country finds its way into the profits column of one of the transnational corporations. The tune played by power may appear to change, but the familiar disharmony of domination inevitably resurfaces. "When Pharaoh saw that there was a respite, he hardened his heart and would not listen to them. . ." Always the return to the initial response of no freedom. And so he stands, stubbornly denying the reality of God's intentions until the sea closes over his army.

After their first hesitation, Israel's first response to the announcement of God's coming action is faith and worship: "And the people believed; and when they heard that the Lord had visited the people of Israel and had seen their affliction, they bowed their heads and worshipped." More than once, however, this response alternates with an opposite response of disbelief and resistance. They are not ready for the long hard struggle ahead. And it takes a while for them to learn that while liberation does promise wholeness and justice, it also demands commitment to a difficult struggle.

In fact, the first effect of God's action is increased hardship for the slaves. Pharaoh increases their workload as a punishment for listening to Moses, and as an inducement to turn away from his preaching.

The response of the powers of the world to demands for justice is nearly always designed to discourage the yearnings of the people for freedom. The object is both to break the spirit of freedom and to create divisions and dissension among the oppressed. For example, there is an argument about South Africa that begins: "But if we disinvest or place economic sanctions on South Africa, the blacks will be the first to suffer and the hardest hit." Of course, the argument has truth in it. The government does have the power to make the weak and powerless suffer. Pharaoh commands that now the Hebrews

44

This is well said. All the same, it may not necessarily be a gesture of humility when the church divests itself of the "vestiges of Empire." Nor is it necessarily an indication of the desire to seek an alternative to the way of Christendom. It may rather be "to everyone's advantage," including the church's. For power does not lie with kings and empires now. The tokens of courtly life and of the old aristocracy no longer benefit the church. It may be only a new bid for proximity to power when churches move to divest themselves of old symbols.

In fact, if Protestantism in North America has been quantitatively successful for longer than Catholicism in Latin Europe, it is partly because Protestantism soon found out the direction in which power had shifted. It went from the palaces of kings to the houses of merchants and highly placed bureaucrats. And for a long time it stayed there.

Can you identify some circumstances in which power has kept itself intact while seeming to accommodate to criticism?

What about Jim Crow laws in the Southern U.S.A.?

The substitution of literacy tests for race as a criterion for voting?

Can you offer some illustrations of your own?

must gather their own straw for making bricks, thus making their work even more difficult than before. And the leaders of the Hebrews were deceived, and blamed Moses for their problems. "The Lord look upon you and judge you because you have made us offensive in the sight of the Pharaoh and his servants, and have put a sword in their hand to kill us."

The worst part about this strategy is that it is so often effective. Oppressed peoples can be kept confused and in their place by having their work increased or decreased by the whimsical will of their oppressor. It makes them look at their oppressive rulers as the only potential benefactor, and it makes them think of freedom seekers among their own people as dangerous trouble makers. Bondage and oppression break the human spirit. It makes people into slaves. It destroys their capacity to seek freedom. From the most individual level to the most corporate level, anyone who has worked for human liberation has experienced what Moses experienced.

Thus, there are two goals—and not just one—to be achieved by God in the task of setting Israel free. Besides the stripping of the oppressor's power to hold the people in bondage, there is the second task of re-awakening the Hebrew people's desire and commitment for wholeness and freedom. In this people, whose enslavement has made them docile and submissive, God the liberator instills, inspires in exact correlation with each other. It was, on the one hand, possible for an individual Hebrew to be "free" while living under Pharaoh's tyrannical rule. Maintaining an un-enslaved mind and spirit while under oppression is always seen as a revolutionary act of resistance. On the other hand, it was possible for Israel to move as a corporate people toward freedom even though not all the Israelites were ready for it. In fact, it is in the Wilderness, following the successful corporate struggle for political liberation, that God's attention really turns to the question of building a truly free people—on individual and collective levels.

God the Actor: Forming and Shaping A People

In the Biblical version of the human drama, liberation does not lead directly into the Promised Land. The Exodus leads

46

"... the real criticism begins in the capacity to grieve because that is the most visceral announcement that things are not right. Only in the empire are we pressed and urged and invited to pretend that things are all right ... And as long as the empire can keep the pretense alive that things are all right, there will be no real grieving and no serious criticism.

"But think what happens if the Exodus is the primal scream that permits the beginning of history."

Walter Brueggemann, *The Prophetic Imagination*.

A basic initial step of freedom is the understanding that whoever or whatever holds us in bondage cannot provide us with what we really need. Conversely, the root of dominance is the notion that the master is really the source of Good for us. For just this reason, slave holders frequently forbid slaves from praying to God for daily bread, so that they would never stop looking to the slave holder for their daily sustenance.

For this, the slave holders set themselves up as God to the slaves. For "A God is whatever you look to as the source of good."

rather to the wilderness and a long wandering pilgrimage. That is the story told in the Book of Numbers. The people of Israel's first experience of freedom is in the desert, and it is a rugged freedom indeed!

This wilderness period in Israel's history is frequently referred to as a time of temptation and testing. God seems to deliberately make the people struggle and fall, setting up roadblocks at every turn, making things as difficult as possible. However, it would be more accurate to see the wilderness not as a place of testing, but as a place of formation—the formation of a people of God. In the wilderness, people who have been relieved of bondage are now to be shaped into a free people.

The image of life as a pilgrimage is in many ways far more realistic to our own lives than any other image. From beginning to end, from life to death, from cradle to the grave, we experience life as a journey. It is also in the context of life as a pilgrimage that we have some of our most important experiences with God the actor. Here is God as we know him, or at least as God would most like to be known by us. Like the people of Israel, our initial act of liberation which we celebrate in our Baptism, does not presume our arrival in the land of milk and honey. Rather it signifies the beginning of a journey through life in which we will be formed and shaped as God's people.

This is not only our experience as individuals, but is also a familiar experience for nations. Following the initial event which brings a nation into being, whether it be a revolution or a peaceful declaration, there is usually a long period of shaping and internal development of the people. This can be illustrated in the experience of the United States, as well as in the contemporary examples of such nations as China, Cuba, Kenya, etc. In fact, few nations experience a lengthy period where they have "arrived" at a final shape of development, before they begin to decline, before they begin a movement—slowly or rapidly—toward their disintegration.

In the case of Israel, as well as in the case of many others in history, the mission of the creating God continues by the forming and shaping of the people he has liberated. A people with a slave consciousness and an extended period of

It is important to understand that the opposite of the slave is *not* the master, but the free person. Masters and slaves are in a reciprocal relationship. Masters are *not* free; they are dependent on the slaves. Just as the slaves lose their humanity by being dominated, so the masters lose their humanity in dominating. It does no good—especially for the slaves—for the slaves to become masters.

What the Hebrews are to become upon leaving Egypt is Israel, not Egypt!

To picture life as a journey is not especially original, it's been done throughout human history. But there are different kinds of journeys. Three come to mind:

A *wandering* which is characterized by aimlessness, meandering, lack of direction. It is going nowhere.

A *quest* which is characterized by compulsive pursuit of the goal. The journey is to be gotten over as rapidly as possible. It is at best a necessary evil.

A *pilgrimage* which is going somewhere, but the "somewhere" is already present in the journey itself. Sometimes a pilgrimage can be confused with a quest. It has a goal. Sometimes a pilgrimage can be confused with a wandering because it takes frequent detours.

If life is a wandering, God is simply absent. If life is a quest, God is simply absent. If life is a quest, God is at the end. If life is a pilgrimage God journeys with us toward his Kingdom.

Can you perceive of your life individually and in family—as a pilgrimage?

Can you describe some of the elements of your pilgrimage?

Can you see both "provision" and "limitation"?

Can you honestly say it is pilgrimage rather than quest or wandering?

brokenness and suffering must now be transformed into a free people of justice and rightness. The slave consciousness of the past focused mainly on survival, the very need to remain alive. In such a situation, submission to bondage becomes a necessity; reducing of risk and conserving of each ounce of life's energies is the highest priority. By contrast, the act of being created into a new and free people calls for willing risk and the commitment of all of life's energies toward the future, and for the giving of one's self to serve the people.

To carry out this task of converting Hebrew slaves into liberated Israel, God does two things in the wilderness: God provides and God limits. God provides: food, water, leadership, guidance by day and night, a covenant, a system of laws. All that is necessary for the people to survive and grow is provided by the one who promises to be with them forever. At the same time, implicit in everything that God provides is a limitation, a boundary designed to define and qualify the content of peoplehood.

That which symbolizes most clearly this providing and limiting action of God is the daily food, the "manna" eaten by the people. Each day the manna appears, to take care of the people's hunger; it is always enough to satisfy, but never too much. The manna, God's "enough" always gets distributed equally:

> ". . .they gathered, some more, some less. But
> when they measured it . . . those that gathered
> much had nothing over and those who gathered
> little had no lack."

Here there is no playing of one person off against another. An oppressor/slave mentality has one person's success depend upon another person's failure. Where God is the provider, the community shares what God provides in such a way that each receives what they need. It is the promise and the gift of *daily bread*.

The manna's limitation is that it cannot be hoarded. If the daily bread is not eaten, but clutched as insurance against the next day it becomes infested with worms, and it rots. Hoarding is out of the question; even its attempt brings the judgment of God.

All talk of nations is filled with a problem, viz. the modern "nation-state." This political entity, though not much more than 300 years old, so dominates our thinking that we conclude it has always been so. But the fact is that they are relative newcomers to the human scene. They might be looked at as stages on a *people's* pilgrimage to community.

If you think of nations as elements of pilgrimages, can you see the limiting and providing work of God in those stories as you know them from history books? Try to make lists of both limiting and providing activities in the case of the following nations:

The Roman Empire
The British Empire
The United States of America
Cuba

Of course, the people will not always eat manna. Eventually, they will leave the wilderness and settle down in the land called "promised" where they will plant and harvest and raise cattle, when they will eat and be full. But even then, the consciousness of manna will pervade their lives. Even in prosperity they are to keep the consciousness of "enough". Moses is commanded to preserve some manna and keep it for all generations. It is part of God's mission to always remind us that our freedom is sustained by God's provision of enough, and it is limited by his command against hoarding and greed.

But slave consciousness does not die easily. No sooner are the people outside of Pharaoh's domination (about six weeks after the Exodus), and the people begin to complain about their new state of existence. God's "enough" was not enough for people who still had no model of success other than that of the Egyptian oppressor.

> "Would that we had died by the hand of the Lord in the land of Egypt, when we sat by the fleshpots and ate bread to the full." Ex. 13:3

This brings us back again to God's setting of limits, (might be called "judgment") which sometimes takes the form of judgment. In the wilderness God provides enough. But things are not simply changed by an act of the will. So imbedded are the Pharaoh's ways of seeing things that "enough" is seen as "nothing" and "worthless", and "loathsome". Such words are all included in the 21st chapter of Numbers which provides us with a story to demonstrate God's mission of judgment. To speak of a mission of judgment may sound terribly harsh to our ears, but slave consciousness must be put to death if the mind of freedom is to be born.

"Nothing"; "worthless"; "loathsome"; these words are part of the people's complaint about the shape of their freedom. And again, it is the consciousness of Pharaoh that is the source of their temptation.

> "And the people became impatient on the way. And the people spoke against God and against

Deuteronomy proclaims the liberty of enough when it calls upon the people to remember that God ". . . humbled you and let you hunger and fed you with Manna . . . that he might make you know that man does not live by bread alone, but that man lives by everything that proceeds out of the mouth of the LORD."

(Deuteronomy 8:3)

An advertising campaign called "Movin' On To A Better America" calls FREE ENTERPRISE "a natural system that follows the common law of humanity" and "rewards those who work and compete in life and frowns upon those unwilling to justify their own existence . . ."

(*The Progressive*. October 1978, p. 47)

St. Paul writes to the Church in Corinth, "I do not mean that others should be eased and you burdened, but that as a matter of equality your abundance at the present time should supply their want, so that there may be equality. As it is written, "He who gathered much had nothing over and he who gathered little had no lack."

(II Corinthians 8:13-15 cf. Exodus 16:18)

> Moses: 'Why have you brought us out of Egypt
> to die in the wilderness? For there is no food and
> no water and we loathe this worthless food'."
> "Then the Lord sent fiery serpents among the
> people and they bit the people, so that many
> people of Israel died."

Whatever else snakes may signify, they at least tell us in this story that our rejection of life from the hand of God ends up turning back on ourselves with the result that it is we who are consumed. Our desire for affluent and secure slavery does not produce the results that are intended. We do not end up well off, but destroyed.

One interesting thing about this judgment is that on the face of it, it does not need to be seen as judgment. It could be just another natural disaster. Since the story of the garden, snakes have had a connection with evil and catastrophe for people. So perhaps this could be nothing more than a natural disaster. It takes a special sense to see disaster as judgment. It means having to take God seriously, at least seriously enough to believe that God would take the time to judge our infidelity. This means believing that God takes our human life seriously enough to want more from it than the old enslavements that keep us from doing justice and peace in the world.

The very fact that God judges us, that he does not let our actions go without consequence, is a very hopeful word. It is a lifesaving word. It means that God cares enough about lives to have them matter. Left on our own we would probably keep on complaining that we need more and more until, in our exploitation of the earth, we smothered to death in our own garbage. The environmental crisis which now "bites" us may keep us from this fate.

Judgment, once set in motion, is not easily stopped. The snakes did not go away simply because they were recognized as judgment. But in the midst of judgment, salvation is set. Our story recognizes an unusual thing about salvation: it sometimes resembles the judgment itself. One of the snakes—or its image—is placed upon a pole and by the command of God those who look at it survive the deadly bite they have brought upon

You want to be
You want to be,
excuse me,
first get free
of that excess
of goods
which cram
your whole body
leaving no room
for you and even less
for God.

We must have no illusions. We must not be naive. If we listen to the voice of God, we make our choice, get out of ourselves and fight non-violently for a better world. We must not expect to find it easy; we shall not walk on roses, people will not throng to hear us and applaud, and we shall not always be aware of divine protection. *If we are to be pilgrims for justice and peace, we must expect the desert.*

7 The Inevitable desert

55

themselves. The kind of salvation that God offers us—his mission in the midst of judgment—includes confrontation with the truths about ourselves. To pretend that we do not have a slave consciousness within us, to pretend that our lives are not broken, to pretend that we do not participate in the breaking of others, is to condemn ourselves to perpetual enslavement, and to condemn others along with us.

This snake on a pole was seen by Jesus as a model of his own crucifixion. It is a model of salvation that gives us a perpetual reminder that God's mission brings him again and again into the midst of our brokenness, a brokenness which he takes upon himself to restore the creation.

God the Actor: Establishing Just Community

For Christian faith, the focal point of God's mission to restore our humanity and so to save the creation is the life and work of Jesus. In him, all three of the major acts of God already described are fully present. Jesus the Christ is one with the maker and sustainer of life; he is the saviour and liberator; he is at the center of the new community of the people of God.

What's more, in Christ's coming, a fourth and final step is taken in the completion of God's mission: in Christ, the perfect Kingdom of justice and rightness is fulfilled. In his death and resurrection, the last enemy of the creation—death itself—is destroyed: the Kingdom is established and the King of Kings assumes the throne.

But this is no normal king, nor is he simply a triumphalistic magnification of a normal king into a sovereign many times more powerful than has been known before. Rather, in Jesus a just and true king is shown to be one who is a suffering servant. The Kingdom of Heaven, in which all of the brokenness is overcome and all rightness is established, is a Kingdom of caring and serving people who are ruled by a servant/king.

Just before his condemnation and execution, the Gospel according to John reports Jesus' words as he stands before the Roman governor who seemed to hold the power of life and death in his hands. Jesus says to the governor, "My Kingship is

Could it be that the inflationary spiral will turn out to be the saving judgment of God? Inflation comes from the desire to acquire and consume. But the result of that desire (inflation) strikes back at us and destroys us. We are snakebitten. The dollar sags on the international market. U. S. influence is cut back around the globe. Our great power is taken from us. Could it be our salvation?

"God also protects me in time of danger and guards me from every evil."

Martin Luther, Small Catecism

Christian faith confesses the protection of God. But it is not the testing of a contract that is involved. Rather, "All this He does out of fatherly and divine goodness and mercy, though I do not deserve it."

And it is set in the context of God's creative mission, his care for the creation. It is part of what it means to say "I believe in God the Father Almighty, Maker of Heaven and Earth."

not of this world; if it were of this world, my servants would fight that I not be handed over. . ." Too often these words are taken to mean that Jesus is a King in some other place (in heaven? in the future? in our hearts?). But the distinction Jesus is making is *not where* his Kingdom is located; rather he is stating that the *kind of Kingdom* he rules is different from worldly kingdoms. Jesus is redefining what it means to be a king.

The kingship of this world is the sovereignty of the chess board. On the chess board the life of the king is to be defended at all costs. Pawns, knights, bishops, queens, all the other pieces of the board that represent persons, are called upon to sacrifice themselves in order to preserve the king. Even the material world's representative, the rook or the castle, can be "wasted" for his preservation. Such is the way of power and sovereignty of this world. Jesus makes a plain declaration that his kingship is not of this kind. The term "king", when used with respect to Jesus, is transformed by him.

How is it transformed? "This is my son, the beloved, with whom I am well pleased." (Matt. 3:17); "Behold my servant whom I have chosen, my beloved with whom my soul is well pleased," (Isa. 42:1, as quoted in Matt. 12:18); "This is my beloved Son, with whom I am well pleased, listen to him." (Matt. 17:5); "But I am among you as one who serves." (Luke 21:17).

How is the notion of sovereignty transformed by Jesus? It is persistently understood in terms of life-giving service on behalf of wholeness and restoration for broken people in a broken world. The background for all of the verses cited above is the mission statement that appears in Isaiah 42. The mission involved is the mission of God through his servant: "Behold my servant . . . my chosen . . . I have put my spirit upon him." There the nature of the mission is repeated three times:

> ". . . he will bring forth justice
>   to the nations;
> ". . . he will faithfully bring
>   forth justice;
> ". . . he will not fail or be discouraged
>   till he has established justice
>   in the earth."
>   (Isaiah 42:1-4)

Read Luke 4:
  How does Jesus there describe his mission?

  Any government can be understood under the New Testament term king-ship or kingdom. The terms could be rendered by "rule" or "sovereignty" or even "government" itself. In light of that we ought to reflect on the famous and often cited inaugural address of John Kennedy when he said, ". . . Do not ask what your country can do for you, but ask what you can do for your country."

  What does the word country refer to? The government? The people?

Once again the mission of creation is affirmed. The earth, the nations, the coastlands, will have justice restored within their borders and they will be restored as God's creation. The servant carried out the commission to be God's faithful representative on the earth for the sake of the wholeness of the earth, and of the entire creation.

It is just this mission of restoration that is embodied in all of Jesus' activity. Those who are broken in physical illness or injury have their health restored: the lame walk, the blind see, the deaf hear, withered hands are given strength. Such events are not displays of power, designed to convince the skeptical of claims to majesty. They are pure acts of serving love which restore health and open the way to participation in the life of the human community once more. Blind beggars not only see again, they are no longer reduced to the status of beggar. Lepers are are not only made clean, they are put back into the society once more.

Those who are broken in other ways are also made whole. Tax-collectors are accepted into this companionship and it creates the possibility that they can cease their money grabbing: Levi gives up his job and Zacchaeus restores what he has extorted from the people. A woman with a long term hemorrhage, who has not only suffered from the disease but has been taken advantage of by the doctors as well is released from both encumbrances by her contact with this faithful servant of God.

His servanthood ushers in a new age; the age of God's rule, God's sovereignty. It does not lead people out of this world to some other sphere or place, but it restores them as whole people in this world. His "not of the world kingship" nevertheless happens *in the world.*

This work of Jesus to restore the broken is persistently seen as a threat by those who wield power in the broken world. They seem to have a vested interest in preserving the brokenness or at least allowing healing to happen only on their own terms. Both religious and political leaders come to see Jesus' work as subversive to their own regime. Religious leaders resent healings that take place on their special day as if it were an invasion of their private territory. Local political bosses see his

Isaiah 42:1-4
1. Behold my servant, whom I uphold, my chosen, in whom my soul delights; I have put my Spirit upon him, he will bring forth justice to the nations.
2. He will not cry or lift up his voice, or make it heard in the street;
3. a bruised reed he will not break, and a dimly burning wick he will not quench;
he will faithfully bring forth justice.
4. He will not fail or be discouraged till he has established justice in the earth;
and the coastlands wait for his law.

very life as a threat to civil tranquility—law and order as we popularly say. It is precisely his "not of this world" rule in the middle of this world that is the threat. Had he simply been a competitor, playing the game on their terms, living off of the brokenness of others there would have been no problem. We have all seen well enough in our own times how competitors can learn to "cooperate" with each other to keep their strong place in the world secure. But Jesus was no competitor. He was so radically different that he was a complete threat to their regimes.

And he still is. The person of Jesus and the promise to establish the Kingdom of Justice and Rightness continues to represent God's mission as a threat to all the Kingdoms of brokenness and injustice in our world. This is a major reality to keep in mind as we now approach the second half of our study, as we explore our calling to participate in God's mission during our lifetimes.

As we will explore in greater depth, we are first called to receive the gift of God's mission through our participation in the community of believers, the church of Jesus Christ. Second, we are called to join with God in mission by serving sisters and brothers in the world—announcing the Kingdom of Justice and Rightness, and searching for signs of its presence already in our present history.

Part Two

The Participation of the
People in God's Mission

Part II

A. RECEIVERS OF GOD'S MISSION

Introduction

The Church's mission begins: the first and central task of the Christian community as it seeks to join God in mission is to recognize, receive, and celebrate the actions of God in all the world. Hopefully it has been made clear in Part I that God's actions are not aimed exclusively at the Church nor are they received exclusively by the Church. God's actions to restore the creation are provided for the whole world. "The rain falls on the just and unjust alike." But it *is* the exclusive and particular task of the people of God/the Church to be "lookouts" for God's actions taking place, and to make explicitly clear in the Church's proclamation and celebrations that these actions of God take place and are to be received in order to complete the mission to restore the creation to wholeness.

As the results of God's actions are identified by the Church in the events that transpire daily in the world, the faith in the resurrected Lord of history is confirmed and proclaimed. The people of God/the Church give praise for God's continuing *creative activity* as new life is recognized entering unceasingly into the world. The people of God/the Church celebrate the *liberating activity* of God in the never-ending struggles for freedom of those who are in bondage in the world. The people of God/the Church recognize God's *activity of providing and limiting* for all peoples in the world. And the people of God/the Church wait and watch longingly as God's *activity brings the just and perfect Kingdom* closer and closer.

Thus, the internal life of the Christian community, including the personal life of each Christian, is based upon this belief that

64

Taming the New Leviathan—A Task For the Church

While the building of a transnational politics which is open, public, and participatory is so far in the future as to remain utopian, fortunately small beginnings exist. Some transnational church programs, for example, link people who seek alternatives to the models associated with the transnational developmentalist system. Institutes devoted to concerned research abound and are developing Third World ties. Pressure is being applied at a variety of points within the system by groups and individuals working in concert across national borders. Hopefully, more people are becoming critically aware of the nature of the system. Understanding and awareness—"naming" the system—constitute the first steps in transformation, in building a new transnational politics that could begin to tame the New Leviathan.

God's activities are still being received in the world, and that the Church has the special task of identifying these things taking place. In the following pages we shall use three of the most familiar images of "receiving" in the New Testament, as a means of exploring further this "receiving task" of the Church.

The first "receiving image" is Baptism, which is the primary sign for Christians of God's liberating action. Baptism is our Exodus. It is our act of receiving God's mission of freedom.

The second "receiving image" is Holy Communion, which is the celebration of God's providing and limiting for the people of God. The bread and wine of Holy Communion is our manna in the wilderness; it is our receiving of God's "enough" for our journey through life.

The third image is the "receiving" of the Holy Spirit, through which the Church is established as the harbinger of a new humanity and heralds the coming of the just and perfect Kingdom. Under the inspiration of the Holy Spirit, the Christian community is transformed from being "receivers" of God's mission, into those who join and represent God in mission to others.

Baptism: Receiving Our Liberation

For Christians, the entrance into participation in God's mission is our Baptism. In this act of receiving we are changed once again into the people of God. We have seen that God's mission is to be understood in terms of change: nothingness is changed into the creation; slaves are changed into free people; this present age will be changed into the Kingdom of God. If the mission of God is change and the first thing we do with mission is receive it, then it is obvious that the first thing that happens in mission is that *we are changed.*

The goal and central symbolism, therefore, of our Baptism is that we are being changed, are being set free. Baptism is our Exodus, our liberation into life. God changes us and restores us to wholeness in order that we might live. Moreover, this change does not begin and end at the moment of Baptism. Rather, Baptism commits us to a lifetime of being changed.

Romans 6:1-4

What shall we say then? Are we to continue in sin that grace may abound? By no means! How can we who died to sin still live in it? Do you not know that all of us who have been baptized into Christ Jesus were baptized into his death? We were buried therefore with him by baptism into death, so that as Christ was raised from the dead by the glory of the Father, we might walk in newness of life.

What does Baptism give?

It works forgiveness of sins, delivers from death and the devil, and gives eternal salvation to all who believe, as the words and promises of God declare.

It signifies that the old Adam in us should, by daily contrition and repentance, be drowned and die with all sins and evil lusts, and again, a new person daily come forth and arise, who shall live before God in righteousness and purity forever.

Martin Luther—*Small Catechism*

The significance of our baptism can be seen in the story of the tax collector of Jericho, Zaccheus. He is an archetype of human brokenness. Reduced to subservience by the powerful forces of the Roman State, he is then used to exploit his own countrymen, collecting the pound of flesh that Rome extracts and trading in his humanity for a parasitical life that feeds off the oppression of his sisters and brothers, who in turn hold him in contempt.

As the story unfolds his curiosity got him slightly nearer to Jesus than he anticipated and he found himself invaded. Not waiting for an invitation, Jesus invited himself to Zaccheus' home. And the flow of money and goods reversed. "Behold, Lord, the half of my goods I give to the poor; and if I have defrauded anyone of anything, I restore it four fold."

When Zaccheus said "Christ changed my life," he knew what he was talking about, unlike many of us, who say it but really mean, "nothing has changed, but Jesus makes me comfortable with it all."

It may be difficult for contemporary Christians to perceive the idea of our being changed, in the old familiar ritual of Baptism. Even when the form of Baptism is clearly a matter of receiving by passive infants, the rite is likely to be so innocuous that none would suspect that change is involved. A few drops of water neatly placed or perhaps dabbled with a rose bud so as to elicit grand-parental "coos" and congregational smiles without disturbing the neat "christening gown", hardly bespeaks profound change.

Even more to the point, where some reminiscence of the New Testament Baptismal form is kept, as in those churches where it is normal to immerse adults, Baptism is usually seen not as something "received", but rather a "giving" of self by the person baptized. It is a "confession of faith" or "testimony" of *my* actions, *my* accepting Jesus. It is not seen as the dramatic choice of God to act toward me.

And whether a particular church practices infant Baptism or only adult Baptism, is mostly beside the point since *all* churches in this society are popularly seen as voluntary associations in which we choose God rather than our being chosen and freed by God's actions upon us. Like everything else in our consumer society, we are given options to choose from in a supermarket of

"Create in me a new life,
a new life, Spirit born.
Born for caring
and for sharing
To acclaim God
with the light of the dawn."

from "Create in Me," a folk
liturgy by Norman Habel

. . . What the black man says today in southern Africa is the
following: "Understanding Christ's message of love as meaning that
one has to be prepared to meet his neighbor's needs, understanding his
call to turn the other cheek, I am prepared to be detained, tortured,
shocked with electricity, beaten up, shot dead, to be pushed from the
10th floor of the building on John Vorster Square, to be jobless, to be
called a terrorist, communist or even hang, but for the sake of you and
my liberation, for the sake of love, I am not prepared to compromise." I
would rather turn the other cheek.

Ephesians 2:13-16
But now in Christ Jesus you who once were far off have been brought
near in the blood of Christ. For he is our peace, who has broken down
the dividing wall of hostility, by abolishing in his own flesh the law of
commandments and ordinances, that he might create in himself one
new man in place of the two, so making peace, and might reconcile us
both to God in one body through the cross, thereby bringing the
hostility to an end.

competing denominational brands. God sits on a shelf, waiting to be chosen.

The New Testament portrayal is radically different. Baptism is described as nothing less than a matter of death and resurrection. "Do you not know", writes St. Paul, "that as many of us as were baptized into Christ Jesus were baptized in his death?" This is more than an innocent religious name-giving ceremony, more than a confession of faith or testimony. It is in fact our death and burial. What we receive when we receive God's mission of Baptism is the end of our broken lives in death, in order that we can receive new whole life again.

Baptism is a "once for all" event, but it is not a "once and over with" event. Baptism gives us death and resurrection as the perpetual shape of our life as God's people. It is the model of Israel's Exodus into the wilderness, with its rugged freedom, that is thrust upon us. For us too the consciousness of Pharaoh dies with difficulty, and in order to kill it Baptism is our daily way of life. Each day is for Christians a matter of receiving our life from God. We have died and our life is given back to us. Each day is a matter of dying to the old and being raised to new life.

If it is Israel's Exodus that is the model that we are to use in order to see our Baptism aright, then there are a series of affirmations which we must make. Each of them could be the subject of extensive comment, but we won't do that here. Our hope, however, is two-fold: first, this whole book could be seen as comment on the following affirmations; second, readers will take the time to reflect on them and talk about them with their sisters and brothers.

The affirmations are these (we offer them with the presupposition stated in each case):

1. If Israel's Exodus is the proper model for our Baptism, then Baptism is a movement from isolation to community. Sin and/or slavery alienate us from each other, setting us as competitors for life. In Baptism our isolation is put behind us and we are set in cooperative solidarity with the people of God, the Body of Christ.

2. If Israel's Exodus is the proper model for our Baptism, then our Baptism incorporates us into a movement away from

We have previously mentioned a number of movements that have used the term "liberation." Here is a list of some other protests and revolts. Are they genuinely liberating? Are they rooted in God's liberating work?

Tax-Revolt ("proposition 13")

Trucker's Strike

For I received from the Lord what I also delivered to you, that the Lord Jesus on the night in which he was betrayed took bread and when he had given thanks, he broke it, and said, "This is my body which is broken for you."

injustice and the toleration of brokenness and harm to others. Our Baptism does not separate us from other human beings and human communities which struggle for freedom and justice; rather our baptism opens us to see the re-creative significance of all struggles for human life. And the sign that we are baptized will be the cross, our suffering solidarity with all the oppressed.
3. If Israel's Exodus is the proper model for our Baptism, then our Baptism will take us not directly into the Kingdom, but into the wilderness. Baptism places us on a pilgrimage whose goal is the Kingdom of God and whose leader is the God of the Kingdom. The promise made to us as we journey is that we shall be provided with enough, that God will judge us, limit us when we fall back into our old ways of life. In our Baptism, God is committed to be God for us all along the way.

Holy Communion: Manna In the Wilderness

Thrust into the freedom of our Baptismal Exodus, we are formed and shaped along the way. We are a pilgrim people, a people on a journey. Our destination is creation restored and made whole—the Kingdom of God. The Kingdom of God is not some other world, but this world under God's just rule. The Kingdom is our destination. We move toward it; we are not yet there. Having been set free from bondage to Pharaoh's mindset, which impacts both masters and slaves, we are now being formed into what we are: freed people. Our humanity is being restored to us; and at the same time the creation—the world as gift—is being regiven.

It goes by many names: The Last Supper, the Eucharist, Holy Communion, the Lord's Table, the Sacrament of the Altar. It is the central act of the people of God/the Church. It is filled to overflowing with meaning, implications, themes. Each dealing with the Supper leaves yet something unsaid. The Last Supper begs us to reflect again and again on its meaning.

The food of this table is our Manna, our provision for the journey in the wilderness. It is "enough", sufficient for our pilgrimage from Baptismal Exodus to Promised Kingdom. It is God's provision that we receive. The table is always the *Lord's*

"This is what the Lord has commanded: 'Gather of it every man of you, as much as he can eat; you shall take an omer apiece, according to the number of people whom each of you has in his tent.' "

And the people of Israel did so; they gathered some more and some less. But when they measured it with an omer, he that gathered much had nothing left over, he that gathered little had no lack; each gathered according to what he could eat." Exodus 16:16-18

Read II Corinthians chapter 8. Note especially vss. 13-15 "I do not mean that others should be eased and you burdened, but that as a matter of equality your abundance at the present time should supply their want, so that their abundance may supply your want, that there may be equality. As it is written, 'He who gathered much had nothing over, and he who gathered little had no lack.' "

The Eucharist itself becomes at times captive to the broken world.

table, and not ours. It is God's bread, Christ's body given to us: "Take and eat." It is God's cup, Christ's blood given for all. "Take and drink." At this table it is God who is the faithful provider.

As God's provision for us, this supper is the sign of God's presence with us along the way. God too is pilgrim. God does not leave us to journey on our own, but travels the desert with us. The form of this presence traveling with us is the crucified one, Jesus Christ. In our world shaped by injustice and brokenness, the one who provides for our needs has himself tasted need. The one who provides for our life along the way does so in the form of the broken ones.

Moreover, this fellow traveller and provider is also the resurrected one. As our world searches and yearns for wholeness and joy, the one who feeds us with himself, is himself our greatest sign of joyful wholeness. The God who provides for our life on the way does so as the perfect image of restored humanity.

Among the multitude of meaning in our receiving this food and drink, is the theme of our receiving forgiveness. God's mission to restore us to wholeness is carried out again and again as we wander away, become lost, are found and welcomed home again. The wine of communion is often referred to as the "cup of forgiveness."

This regular need of being set back on the right path is not only an individual need for all persons, but it is also the need of the corporate body of the people of God/the Church. Since the Church is also a human institution, it is just as affected by brokenness as all else that is human. The oneness and wholeness of the Church is not all that easy to perceive. More visible are the divisions, the perversions of the Gospel and the yielding to the temptation to be an imitator of the world.

We should not be surprised by this. Such has been the case in every step of Biblical history of God's people—in Egypt, in the Exodus, in the wilderness, in Israel, among the disciples, in the early church. This sinfulness of God's people is not an invalidating of the action of God in the Eucharist. Rather, it was for the very purpose of dealing with these problems of God's people that the Eucharist was instituted.

74

THE EUCHARIST, CAPITALISM AND COLONIALISM

Over the centuries the spirituality of the Eucharist—of giving and not of grabbing—was obliterated. The Eucharist went side by side with the worst and largest-scale exploitation that the world has ever seen. The tragedy of the subordination of Christianity to European power politics was also the tragedy of the Eucharist. As the priests and monks went hand in hand with the colonialists, the Eucharist was desecrated in the service of empire. The Eucharist was (one hopes unconsciously) perverted in the close alliance between imperialism and the church. Gold grabbed from the native people of South America was used to adorn Christian monasteries and churches, as in Lima, Peru. The gold used to decorate the ceiling of the Basilica of Saint Mary Major in Rome is claimed to have been brought from the new territories conquered for the Christian rulers and religion. These are symbols of the low level to which religion had sunk in the Europe of the colonial period. Hence we must not be so naive as to accept as "faith" whatever beliefs or practices prevail at any given time concerning the Eucharist. We must not think that the so-called simple faith of the people is innocent in itself. It has been evolved alongside the world's worst exploitation and did not contest it or, rather, it tended to justify the status quo.

There is not a single human relationship that does not require—time and time again—the patient forgiveness and reacceptance of one person by another. In this forgiveness is the remaking and strengthening of the original relationship. Our receiving forgiveness, our being welcomed back into relationship with God is part and parcel of our being provided with "enough" in the wilderness.

Another theme that is central to the understanding of Holy Communion is that of "remembering". "Do this in remembrance of me" is the command of Christ that is observed as we eat and drink at his table. What is remembered, however, is something far more than the person of Jesus. It is the entire history of God's actions to restore the creation, of which the life, death and resurrection of Christ is the fulfillment. What is remembered is that we are God's people, receiving all that God has given us.

The act of remembering is an important function in the cementing together of all human communities, and especially of the people of God. We remember as we retell all the old stories—over and over and over again—all that God has done throughout history. And as we remember and recall the past, God becomes present to us again in the present. It is more than a play on words to say that as we eat this bread and drink this cup together while *remembering* Christ, he becomes *re-membered* among us, and we ourselves become *members* of his body. Likewise, the words themselves are of great importance when we say that we *receive* God's mission to make us whole again when we receive God in the eating and drinking of this meal he sets before us.

Another word that is used very often in the context of Holy Communion is "celebrating". We "celebrate" the Sacrament of the Altar. Something of the festiveness of the occasion is captured by this word. What's more, in the act of our celebrating, our rejoicing is more than over the memory that God has time and time again in history been the provider and limiter for the people of God. We are also celebrating that this same function is taking place now.

What's more, that which is being celebrated by those who gather around the Lord's Table is the action of God's providing

"Have we not all one father
  Has not one God created us?
  Why then are we faithless to one another, profaning the
covenant of our Fathers?"

Malachi 2:10

Can you relate this prophetic word to our table?
  And fear came upon everyone and many wonders and signs
were done through the apostles. And all who believed were
together and had all things in common; and they sold their
possessions and goods and distributed them to all, as any had
need. And day by day, attending the temple together and
breaking bread in their homes, they partook of food with glad
and generous hearts.

Acts 2:43-46

  Now the company of those who believed were of one heart and
soul, and no one said that any of the things which he possessed
were his own, but they had everything in common. And with
great power the apostles gave their testimony to the resurrection
of the Lord Jesus, and great grace was upon them all. There was
not a needy person among them, for as many were possessors of
lands or houses sold them and brought the proceeds of what was
sold and laid it at the apostles' feet; and distribution was made to
each as any had need.

Acts 4:32-35

  "For as in one body we have many members and all the
members do not have the same function, so we though many are
one body in Christ and individually members one of another.
Having gifts that differ according to the grace given to us, let us
use them . . ."
Romans 12:5-6

Compare I Corinthians 12:4-31

and limiting in all of the world, and not just in this restricted setting. The function of the church to "recognize, receive and celebrate the actions of God in all the world" which was referred to at the beginning of this section, comes fully into play here. The people of God, remembering the promises of God to continue this providing/limiting function in the world, look out into the world to observe and celebrate its taking place at any given moment. Each new harvest, each action of caring and just sharing, each attempt to create new systems of just distribution are celebrated as acts of God providing for the creation. Each exposure of greed and corruption, each collapse and failure of unjust systems, each failure to continue oppression is celebrated as God's limiting judgment.

Thus, when the Christian community gathers around the Lord's table, the celebration is not only a remembering that God has always provided and limited in the past, but that the creation is even now receiving God's provision of "enough".

Finally, at the Communion table, we are not individual consumers; we are receivers of God's gifts as the family of God. Often we treat our churches as voluntary religious associations. We belong to them as individuals as long as we are interested and they provide some personal benefit to us. But the church is family. We have a common parent, God. We have common ancestors: Abraham and Sarah, Moses and Miriam. We have a common elder brother, Jesus, whose faithfulness blesses all our lives. We gather as sisters and brothers around the family table for our daily bread.

And we have family rules among ourselves. One version of these rules is as follows:

"I am the Lord your God who brought you out of Egypt and there will not be any other gods for you. Therefore in this family we do not make any graven images or worship them.

we do not use God's name lightly
we do remember and celebrate the day of our liberation
we do take care of our elderly
we do not kill
we do not commit adultery
we do not steal
we do not lie about each other or tear each other down
we do not covet what belongs to another

Kumbaya my Lord, kumbaya
Kumbaya my Lord, kumbaya
Kumbaya my Lord, kumbaya
O Lord, kumbaya.

Someone's crying Lord, kumbaya,
Someone's crying Lord, kumbaya,
Someone's crying Lord, kumbaya,
O Lord, kumbaya.

Someone's singing Lord, kumbaya,
Someone's singing Lord, kumbaya,
Someone's singing Lord, kumbaya,
O Lord, kumbaya.

African Song Kumbaya

Another ancient version—this time from the Christian branch of the people of God—went like this:
"Bless those who curse you
pray for your enemies
if someone deprives you of your property, do not ask for it back
do not murder
do not commit adultery
do not corrupt boys
do not fornicate
do not steal
do not practice sorcery
do not murder a child by abortion or kill a newborn infant
do not covet your neighbor's property
do not commit perjury
do not bear false witness
do not hate anybody; but reprove some, pray for others and still others love more than your own life.
do not associate with the high and mighty but be with the upright and humble.
do not turn your back on the needy, but share everything with your brother and call nothing your own."
Clearly teachings such as this are not divorced from our celebration. In our teaching we learn the stories and songs and actions that make up our celebrations and we reflect on the meaning of our world in light of our celebration. We even get to practice our celebration.

And we get to practice the actions of caring and serving, giving and receiving that embody our family values. "Do good to all people; especially those who are of the family of faith." That is the injunction laid upon us by the apostle. It is not so much that we love our sisters and brothers in the faith *more* as it is that we love them *first*. It is not that we receive God's mission from them *alone*, but that we receive it from them first. It is within the household of faith that we are prepared to be givers and receivers, sharers and participants. Here we receive the "foretaste" of brokenness made whole, discover the model of creation restored.

Our family is not without tension, but a life in which brokenness is transcended in forgiveness and acceptance and

In the following space take the time to write out your own version of family dos and don'ts. Remember that they are not rigid laws to be enforced by violence, but are the embodiment of the values that come from a family whose story is about the liberation that comes from God.

. . . as I reflect on ministry, and especially my ministry, I know in the hidden places that the real restraints are not in my understanding or in the receptivity of other people. Rather, the restraints come from my own unsureness about this perception. I discover that I am as bourgeois and obdurate as any to whom I might minister. I, like most of the others, am unsure that the royal road is not the best and the royal community the one which governs the real "goodies." I, like most of the others, am unsure that the alternative community inclusive of the poor, hungry, and grieving is really the wave of God's future.

Walter Brueggemann
The Prophetic Imagination, p. 111

mutual service. It is not a life without struggle, but a life of common struggle, of struggling together. If we are the church and not a sect we are a "motley crew" of different ages, sexes, races, opinions and resources. But those differences are "reconciled;" that is, they are put at the service of others in the community. Rather than being barriers to keep us apart or instruments by means of which we exploit one another, our gifts become the points of contact with other people and our means of serving them and caring for their lives. Here we begin to find that our gifts are not fulfilled when they are self-possessed, but that they achieve their purpose when we use them as freely as they have been given to us.

Here we also begin to see that our trust life is not a matter of being self-sufficient but that we *live* in a radical interdependence. None of us has all the gifts—and that not by accident but by God's design. Nor are any giftless if we can look at them as people and not "production units." Here is the beginning of a lived version of justice: each one valued for what they are, and receiving what they need for their enhancement. In its mutual service the church is intended to be a microcosm of God's promise for the coming Kingdom: peoples, lands, nations, all a part of one human family, but each with their own gift and resources to share. When justly shared, the gifts of each are used for the life of all. In Holy Communion we receive a vision of what God intends for all.

Receiving the Holy Spirit

In receiving the Gospel, God's mission, the people of God receive the Holy Spirit. The Holy Spirit is not, however, something in addition to our baptism and the gift we receive at the table; rather, the Holy Spirit is the content of these other events.

There is much popular confusion about the Spirit in our contemporary religious culture, mostly the result of reducing the Gospel to a private matter between God and the individual. Some current talk about the Spirit puts it forward as the religious version of getting "high," a euphoric feeling good in

Simple Gifts

Tis a gift to be simple
Tis a gift to be free
Tis a gift to come down where you ought to be
And when you find yourself in a place just right
Twill be in a garden of truth and delight.

When true simplicity is learned
To bow and to bend we shan't be ashamed.
For to turn, turn, will be our delight
Till by turning, turning we'll come out right.

which common cares, concerns, worries and frustrations are put aside. In this version of Spirit-talk, what the American drug culture promised, the spirit of God is seen to deliver. "It makes me feel so good. I'm so at peace," we hear people say, crediting God with their sense of well-being.

Others speak of the Spirit as the guarantee of their individual success. Spirit is given credit for closing business deals, arranging promotions and providing information otherwise not available. Spirit arranges meetings, produces strange forms of speaking and ecstasy and entering into minds to make correct decisions.

Still others seem to think of the Spirit as a vague but powerful force, something akin to an electric charge. To receive the Spirit is like putting your finger into a light socket. Frequently terms like "mystery" or "mysterious" are employed in such a way as to indicate that spirit is a spooky, incomprehensible affair. People will say things like, "Well, I can't put it into words, but when you feel it, you'll know it."

But things with the Spirit are not so lacking in definition as all of that. *That* the Spirit should be at work in the world may be incomprehensible, but *what* the Spirit is up to is clear enough.

The Spirit is the God of Jesus Christ, the God whose kingdom is justice, peace and joy reaching into this broken world to restore it to the wholeness of the Kingdom. Never amorphous or spooky, the presence of the Spirit is as concrete as the announcement that our sins have been forgiven and that we are freed from the burdens of the past. Never vague, the Spirit is as specific as the martyrs of ancient or modern days who have offered up their lives on behalf of their sisters' and brothers' liberty. "Greater love has no one than this: that they lay down their life for their friends." And there are some occasions when faithful love converts enemies to friends by laying life down even for them. Just that specific and concrete is the Holy Spirit.

Spirit is the power of the gospel word to change our broken, self-centered lives, making them whole once again by breaking down the walls that divide human beings and the walls of race, class, sex, fear, injustice, and exploitation and restoring us to our sisters and brothers.

Most frequently words like comfort, calm, contentment are used to describe Spirit's impact on the world. But there is at least

Record your own language about the Spirit. When do you talk about Spirit? When you do, what kinds of words do you use?

How would you describe the difference between the sense of well-being produced by a drug and the result of Christian conversion? Is there a qualitative difference or merely different sources?

another side to things that we need to reckon with. "No one puts new wine into old wineskins. If they do, the wine will burst the skins and the wine is lost and so are the skins. . . ."

That points to the paradox of our life. Spirit is new, effervescent, heady, power-laden wine. The verbal connection between Holy Spirit and alcoholic "spirits" is no mere accident. Holy Spirit is a mighty intoxicant. Spirited people are "drunk" on justice, liberty, peace, and the care of God's creation and their brothers and sisters. Spirit is new wine.

But this Spirit and spirited people do not appear in heaven or in the kingdom. Rather, they appear in this world: this *old, broken* world. They appear in old wineskins. For just this reason their presence is a threat to the stability, "good order," and present arrangements. The old wineskins of any and every established order do not have the capacity to hold new wine. Discontent with everything less than the Kingdom's justice; ill-at-ease when anyone is oppressed; uncomfortable with the exploitation of any others; restlessness of those who receive and bear the Spirit's peace in a world that is not yet the Kingdom of God. Having had their appetite whetted at the Spirit's table, their yearning is for the last, great table.

Of course, if all that happened was that the new wine was poured into old wineskins, then not only would the old skins be ruptured, but the wine itself would be lost. So, within the old order, new wineskins need to be created. And the spirit is also about that activity. Just as Spirit-filled word calls forth life-filled creation in Genesis, so the Spirit re-creates a life-filled creation providing the new wineskins that spirit can and will fill.

If we can keep ourselves from identifying the term "church" with our present church institutions or some particularly "religious" life, we could say that the Spirit creates the church—the new humanity.

This work of the Spirit is characteristically seen in the gifts and fruits of the Spirit which appear in the New Testament. Lists of Spirited gifts appear in several versions and in several contexts of the New Testament. Sometimes they appear in terms of personages, or roles or perhaps even offices in the body of Christ. So for example, in I Corinthians 12 and Ephesians 4, the gifts are listed as "apostles, prophets, teachers," and so on.

Luke 4 records one version of what it meant for Jesus to be the recipient of the Spirit:
"The Spirit of the Lord is upon me, because he has anointed me to preach good news to the poor.
He has sent me to proclaim release to the captives and recovering of sight to the blind, to set at liberty those who are oppressed, to proclaim the acceptable year of the Lord."

There is neither Jew nor Greek,
there is neither slave nor free,
there is neither male nor female;
for you are all one in Christ Jesus.

Galatians 3:28

On other occasions the gifts seem to be spoken of more as functions. Again, by way of example, in Romans 12 and earlier in I Corinthians 12, we find the gifts listed as "prophecy, various tongues . . . , service, . . . teaching," . . . etc.

A similar listing of "fruits of the Spirit" in Galatians 5, offers what appear to be almost personal virtues. There are "love, joy, peace, patience" and so on.

But whether we encounter gifts or fruits, whether we see virtues or functions, one thing is clear: in all the contexts the gifts are given for the building up of the community. The offices are not stations of prestige. The functions are not ecstatic experiences for a believing elite. The virtues are not merely marks of a personal piety. In each existence what is at stake is the communal life of the church, the exemplary life of the new exemplary humanity. The spirited gifts are the elements of healing in our otherwise fragmented human life.

It should not come as a surprise to find that the gifts mentioned in the Bible, as items in themselves, are not exclusively Christian, but find their counterparts—though all too often in the form of parody—in all human societies. Consider some representative items from the two lists in I Corinthians 12 by way of example. The right side of the page will give you opportunity to extend the examples for yourself.

One of the gifts mentioned is *wisdom*. It does not sound very exciting or ecstatic and indeed it isn't. It is a very mundane gift. It has to do with very practical decisions like where resources will be allotted, or with which other communities will we work co-operatively and which shall we oppose. "Wisdom" happens in pursuit of alliances or in the development of economic policies. Clearly such a practice is not limited to the community of faith and spirit. What makes the gift the Spirit's wisdom is that it pursues the well-being of the whole community.

Healing seems a somewhat more spectacular gift. Perhaps that is why our society seems to have a constant parade of so-called "faith-healers" in the public limelight while "faith-wise people," are limited to more marginal positions. Fortune tellers, palm readers, "advisors" and the like are mostly side-street and back alley types in our world. Again, every society has its authorized healers: shamans, witchdoctors,

Because things in this world of exploding wine skins are rarely clear cut, the church is given the gift and task of "discernment" so that they can make decisions about ambiguous events, movements and persons. Think about the following list of people and on the basis of what you have heard from the news media (or other information about the person that you can gather) try to "discern" the particular gift that they exercise and whether it is done spiritlessly or with the spirit.

"Prophecy" means preaching. Can you think of examples of that function *outside* of the Churches, either in our society or other societies?
What is the task of true preaching?
How does it serve the Community?

Teaching is one of the gifts with obvious equivalents in all human societies. How does your school system measure up when spirit is used as a criterion for evaluating its teaching?
Does the way in which the spirit uses teaching have anything to say about Western dominated third world education which trains people to leave the villages and rural areas and go to cities where they can use their training—medicine, business, engineering—to rise to the top level of the economy, while the village remains resourceless?

Administration basically means "direction giving". Could we venture an example of both spiritless and spirited administration?

herbalists, surgeons, psychiatrists all fill the bill depending on time and place.

What would make a healing spirit-less or spirited? Jesus himself, as the characteristic spirited healer, points the way. Not only does he cure a leper, restore life to a dead girl or sight to a blind man. He also restores them to community. Lepers fulfill their community duties, young girls are given to caring parents, blind men become fellow travellers with the rest of the disciples. Spirited healing not only makes people "better," it restores them to their sisters and brothers.

Demonstration of power or *miracles* is another gift on the list. We use the word today in almost the same way. We speak of the miracles of science and technology and even grant them a religious aura, looking to them to save us from danger or trouble or poverty or perhaps just inconvenience. Indeed, science has become for us the focus of the demonstration of power. We amaze ourselves with people on the moon, gigantic nuclear power plants, over-kill bombs and the like.

But most of our demonstrations of power only enhance the power of the already powerful. The hand of monopolistic power companies is strengthened against their customers. Scientists increase their capacity to do research that perhaps satisfies curiosity but does little else besides enhance the prestige of science. The mad bombers of the military establishments on both sides of the U.S.-Soviet split increase in their ability to turn the world into a terrorists' playground. Just so, we have a spiritless power.

In the New Testament *the miracle of the demonstration of God's Power* is the cross. It is not power consolidated, or exercised as force on behalf of the powerful one, rather it is power given away, manifest as weakness and shown to be on behalf of the life of the world. Such is the nature of spirited demonstrations of power.

As a final example, let us look at the matter of ecstatic speech or in common parlance *"speaking in tongues."* Outbursts of this kind occur not only in the great arena of religion. They appear throughout our social life, perhaps most notoriously in political life. "Sieg Heil," "Better dead than Red," and "Anti-revolutionary reactionary" are examples of such speech which can

The Church of Jesus Christ

The church of Jesus Christ
  is where old women come to dance
    where young men see visions and old men dream dreams
      where children of God bring their balloons.

The church of Jesus Christ
  is where lepers come to be touched
    where the blind see and the deaf hear
      where the lame run and the dying live.

The church of Jesus Christ
  is where the daisies bloom out of barren land
    where children lead and wise men follow
      where mountains are moved
        and walls come tumbling down.

The church of Jesus Christ
  is where loaves of bread are stacked in the sanctuary to
  feed the hungry
    where coats are taken off and put on the backs of the
    naked
      where shackles are discarded and kings and
        shepherds sit down to life together.

The church of Jesus Christ
  is where barefoot children run giggling in procession
    where the minister is ministered unto
      where the anthem is the laughter of the congregation
      and the offering plates are full of people.

(con'd. on page 93)

raise emotion to a fever pitch, while saying nothing of sense to the mind. Political sloganeering regularly works that way and patriotic songs, especially those with military rhythms, work in the same fashion. What they say usually ranges from nonsense, through banal, to crude and sometimes downright cruel. Their ability to stir our emotions is not diminished for all their foolishness or cruelty.

There are other forms of ecstatic speech in our society which are more destructive. You might think of the odd language that binds a cheering section together at a high school basketball game or the language spontaneously invented by a pair of lovers, as an example.

Where speech is spirited as well as ecstatic it serves a dual purpose. On the one hand, like all the gifts it builds community, just as it binds lovers together. On the other hand—perhaps just because it binds the community together!—it confuses and puzzles those who seek the fragmentation and division of the community. Reflection on the spirituals and blues music in the American black community will reveal the powerful nature of spirited ecstatic speech within North American history. This music, most often incomprehensible to whites and labeled vulgar and primitive, preserved human dignity for blacks in the midst of oppressive conditions, and led not a few slaves to freedom.

If these gifts are not, as phenomenon, the peculiar possession of the church, what criteria can be used in a circumstance to identify the Spirit source of the gift? We have tried to say that the communal context of all the passages in question provides the clue. The fruits of the Spirit do not appear as the idiosyncratic virtues of moral superstars or religious elites, but as the way in which the simple command "You shall love your neighbor as yourself," is fulfilled (cf Galatians 5).

In every context, the gifts of the Spirit are seen as the way in which the Body of Christ, the new human Community, is built up and knit together. Not individual exaltation but mutual service is the hallmark of the Spirit's gifts. Each gift is given not for the sake of the recipient, but for the sake of the whole community.

The church of Jesus Christ
  is where people go when they skin their knees or their
    hearts
    where frogs become princes and Cinderella dances
      beyond midnight
      where judges don't judge
        and each child of God is beautiful and precious.

The church of Jesus Christ
  is where the sea divides for the exiles
    where the ark floats and the calf lies down with the lion
      where people can disagree and hold hands at the
        same time.

The church of Jesus Christ
  is where night is day
    where trumpets and drums and tambourines declare
      God's goodness where lost lambs are found.

The church of Jesus Christ
  is where people write thank-you notes to God
    where work is a holiday
      where seeds are scattered and miracles are grown.

The church of Jesus Christ
  is where home is
    where heaven is
    where a picnic is communion and people break bread
      together on their knees.

The church of Jesus Christ
  is where we live responsively to his coming
    Even on Monday morning the world will hear an
      abundance of alleluias and every day is a festival of
        faith!

                              by Ann Weems

B. JOINING GOD IN MISSION IN ALL THE WORLD

Introduction

An ancient symbol of the church is a ship on the ocean. The ocean represents the world in which we live—sometimes calm, life-giving, peaceful; sometimes stormy, merciless, deadly. We are passengers on the ship which is the church. Our voyage is at times calm and lifegiving—an experience of creative discovery and joy. It is also at times dangerously stormy—a fear-filled engagement with enemies in dangerous waters.

Our contemporary times provide an alternative set of symbols which also involve a ship. The world—not the church alone, but all the earth—is a ship. We are all passengers on spaceship earth, riding through the ocean of time and space. The careful arrangement and ecological balance of our relationships on board this ship are constantly being thrown off by our misuse of each other and disregard for the ship's purpose and direction.

So you think that
So you think that
because of her weaknesses,
Christ will forsake her?
The worse his church and ours
is marred by our failures,
the steadier he will support her
with his tender care.
He could not deny
his own body.

Dom Helder Camara

Our contemporary times have also called into being a number of movements within and on the edge of the churches, movements which are formed with the realization that joining God in mission need not wait for the entire institution of the church to provide the initiative for action.

The Civil Rights Movement was one of these; the protest movement against the war in Vietnam was another. The house church movement in the U.S. is small, but quietly strong. Another newer movement that is international in scope is called Christians for Socialism.

In Latin America, people everywhere are joining small action/reflection groups as part of a "base community" movement. They are having a tremendous effect on the church. One of their supporters is Archbishop Dom Helder Camara of Recife, Brazil. He calls such groups in Latin America and all over the world "Abrahamic Minorities."

Turn to page 97.

Our continuing safety and survival on this voyage depend on the successful restoration of justice and peace among the ship's passengers.

The church in such a symbolic representation could be imagined as a wandering community of actors who are concerned about why and where the spaceship is going, and who do improvisational theater with the goal of bringing people to awareness of, and into accord with the ship's direction and purpose.

Whichever of these images seems more fitting to you, or whatever other symbol of the church you might prefer, we are a people joining in and cooperating with God in those actions of God in the world which we have been describing in previous sections of this study. We are the people of God who have received and celebrated God's mission, and now become participants in it. We who have received the Body of Christ have now become the Body of Christ. We are his hands and his feet, his continuing life in the world. We are now a principal means by which God's healing intervention is carried out in a broken world.

It is at this point where it is most crucial that we do not sell short the concept of Christian mission. It is also the point where it is most dangerously possible to do so. The mission of a Christian is all too often seen simply as that of becoming a faithful and useful member of a Christian congregation, attending worship, serving on committees, and helping keep the ship of the church afloat. These are important tasks, but they do not begin to describe the fullness of a Christian's mission. Nor is it sufficient to speak of mission—as so often also happens—in narrowly defined concepts of "evangelism": telling others about Christ, bringing about their conversion, and making them members of the church. These, too, are important tasks, but they represent an incomplete definition of evangelism and are not anywhere near the fullness of Christian mission.

Christian mission is no less sweeping and thoroughgoing than the realization that *everything* a person does is intended to be an act of participation with God in mission in the world. Every act of vocation, avocation, personal relations, private endeavor,

ABRAHAMIC MINORITIES UNITE!

. . . And although I now realize that it is virtually useless to appeal to institutions as such, everywhere I go—and intuitively I include the East—I find minorities with the power for love and justice which could be likened to nuclear energy locked for millions of years in the smallest atoms and waiting to be released . . .

We are told that Abraham and other patriarchs heard the voice of God. Can we also hear the Lord's call? Isn't it pretentious to say this? Dangerously presumptuous?

We live in a world where millions of our fellow men live in inhuman conditions, practically in slavery. If we are not deaf we hear the cries of the oppressed. Their cries are the voice of God . . .

It is not difficult to hear God's call today in the world about us. It is difficult to do more than offer an emotional response, sorrow and regret. It is even more difficult to give up our comfort, break with old habits, let ourselves be moved by grace and change our life, be converted . . .

For the Abrahamic minorities, setting out means to get moving and help many others get moving to make the world juster and more human. . .

It is urgent that we should all unite to denounce and overcome fear. Those who have nothing fear they can do nothing about it, those who have much fear that their goods will be taken away from them.

There are minorities everywhere with the same desire. It would be easy to give further examples, among workers, peasants, journalists, soldiers etc . . . . There are Abrahamic minorities everywhere who are only waiting for the signal to begin and to unite.

If you feel you belong in spirit to the family of Abraham do not wait for permission to act. Don't wait for official action or new laws. The family of Abraham is more a spirit than an institution, more a life style than an organization. It requires the minimum of structure and refers merely to several general principles.

Forgive me if I disturb your peace of mind. But why not ask yourself today, without wasting time deciding whether you have received little or much, whether you have been given the wonderful but awkward, great but dangerous vocation to serve humanity as a member of the Abrahamic minorities?

Excerpts from *The Desert Is Fertile,* Dom Helder Camara (Orbis, Maryknoll, NY, 1976)

public welfare or political activity—*everything* a Christian does ought to have as its purpose the fulfillment of God's creation and an extension of God's bringing wholeness to a broken world.

Mission is far more than doing "Christian" things, although there are some specific actions I take only because I am a Christian (i.e., participation and cooperation in achieving "distributive justice" in a world which the small minority use savage and violent force to prevent the majority from having enough. For Christians in North America, we are called above all else to learn what it means to be "limited", and to struggle against systems which provide too much for us at the expense of others.

Fourth, mission means being aware that all these activities—creating, liberating, providing/limiting—are themselves signs of a new reality that is coming into being: the Kingdom of Justice and Rightness that God has promised. Joining God in the mission of preparing for this eternal kingdom is not an other-worldly task. We do not look for its signs in the heavens or in the supernatural. We look for its signs in the world, in acts of love and justice of brothers and sisters. Learning to be a Christian in mission, therefore, does not mean leaving the world alone and spending as much time as possible in church. Rather it means learning to see and hear the world with new eyes and ears, and to be in the world—as was Jesus—with a new purpose and style. Thus, this concluding portion of our study is not an exploration of our relationship with the church, but rather an exploration of our relationship as Christians with the world.

A. THE WORLD AS FRIEND AND ENEMY

Thus we return to the same theme with which we began at the beginning of this book: the directions we take in our mission with God in the world depend upon our beliefs and attitudes about the world. As we have already seen, there is a tremendous difference of opinion among Christians in their understanding of the world. Some go forth holding their noses and watching

Which of the following can be said to be fulfilling Christian mission? Which cannot? Why?

Teaching a Sunday School Class;
Teaching a public school class;
Feeding the hungry;
Working in a furniture factory;
Designing a railroad bridge;
Constructing a railroad bridge;
Working in a napalm factory;
Serving in the army;
Using napalm in Vietnam;
Washing dishes;
Going to a ballgame;
Adopting a child;
Reading Karl Marx;
Reading Playboy;
Working on an assembly line;
Painting a picture;
Picketing a racist business;
Lobbying for lower taxes;
Refusing to pay war taxes.

Make a list of the things you did yesterday that had something to do with joining God in mission.

Make a list of things your congregation did last year that were a part of Christ's mission. Make a list of those things your congregation did that were not a part of mission.

their purses, helping people to escape while there's still time before God comes to judge and destroy it all. Others go out filled with energy and excitement, designing great programs to change and rebuild the world in God's name. Still others feel almost comfortable with the world the way it is, finding a niche wherever they go that is good to be in and giving God thanks.

Here is a paradox: all these understandings of the world and of our relationship to it, are a part of the total picture of scripture. The problem arises when any one of these deny the validity of the others. As we have already seen, the created world is simultaneously God-made and good, broken and evil, and in the process of being reconciled and made whole. God is, as we have also seen, acting in the midst of all three of these realities; and we are called to do the same.

An even more complicating factor is that in Scripture, the word and image of "world" is used to describe both friendly and enemy territory, and it is impossible to know automatically when one sees the "world" in the Bible, which of these is being referred to without looking at the context in which it is written. Thus, we are faced with the apparent confusion of being sent into the "world" which is good, and at the same time are being told to stay away from the "world" because it is evil.

The "world" is on the one hand always good, always loved by God, whether in the process of being created or in the process of being redeemed and reconciled. On the other hand, the image of "world" is also used to describe evil, and the territory of the "enemy," Satan. The "world" refers to that part of reality which is under the rulership of principalities and powers of darkness. Its values are selfishness and greed. Christians are called upon to do battle against this world, to arm ourselves in opposition to it, to resist, and to refuse to conform to it.

The task of mission with God in the world requires us to be able to discern between these "friendly" and "enemy" territories, to be able to perceive how God's activity responds to them, and to know how to respond to them ourselves as participants in God's actions. Whether we picture ourselves on a ship sailing in and out of friendly waters, as a pilgrim people moving across a desert wilderness from oasis to oasis, or if we

For God so loved the world that he gave his only Son, that whoever believes in him should not perish but have eternal life. For God sent the Son into the world, not to condemn the world, but that the world might be saved through him.

John 3:16, 17

I have come as light into the world, that whoever believes in me may not remain in darkness. If any one hears my sayings and does not keep them, I do not judge him; for I did not come to judge the world but to save the world.

John 12:46, 47

You are the light of the world. A city set on a hill cannot be hid. Nor do men light a lamp and put it under a bushel, but on a stand, and it gives light to all in the house. Let your light so shine before men, that they may see your good works and give glory to your Father who is in heaven.

Matthew 5:14-16

Do not love the world or the things in the world. If any one loves the world, love for the Father is not in him. For all that is in the world, the lust of the flesh and the lust of the eyes and the pride of life, is not of the Father but is of the world. And the world passes away, and the lust of it; but he who does the will of God abides for ever.

I John 2:15-17

Do not be conformed to this world but be transformed by the renewal of your mind, that you may prove what is the will of God, what is good and acceptable and perfect.

Romans 12:2

If the world hates you, now that it has hated me, before it hated you. If you were of the world, the world would love its own; but because you are not of the world, but I chose you out of the world, therefore the world hates you.

John 15:18, 19

dispense with the metaphors and address ourselves as residents in the reality of twentieth century cities and suburbs, we are the people of God in the world seeking to discover and join with God in the process of tearing down and building up, of binding and setting free. To do this requires our developing the ability to identify the good and the evil in the real worlds in which we live.

Friend Or Enemy? The Strong and the Weak

The problem is that there has been an almost complete turnabout between the early Christians and the churches of today in identifying the major areas of friendly and enemy territory in the world. For Jesus and the early church it was a fairly obvious and common assumption that the state—the rulers, authorities, governmental and related systems—would oppose Christianity and its beliefs. The "rulers of this age" were often considered representatives of the principalities and powers of darkness which are under the control of the "enemy" Satan. What's more, the popular and civil religions—the state churches of that day—were included in the category of "enemy territory"; it was assumed that they would almost automatically reject and oppose the Christian faith. This does not mean that the early church was anarchistic. They did advocate obedience to governmental authorities insofar as possible, but they did not assume the possibility of a relationship of friendly alliance and trust between Christians and the state.

On the other hand, "friendly territory" for Jesus and the early church was found among the company of society's outcasts: the poor, sick, oppressed, ignorant and powerless. Not only was this a "safety area" where opposition to Christianity's ideas would not be as strong; it was also the milieu in which the seed of the Kingdom could be planted and be expected to take root.

This should not be interpreted as saying that Jesus was a simple-minded idealist who found no fault among poor and oppressed peoples. He expected no less sin among the outcasts than from anyone else. And he also sought and found good individuals among the rich and educated. It is quite clear,

Different religious traditions have different ways of responding in mission to a "signs" of good and evil in the world. Which of the following are good, evil, or neutral according to what you were taught?

beer	wealth
guns	poverty
police	sex
the pope	movies
communism	dancing
the Masons	religious statues
the military	thriftiness
	anger

Christians and their pastors should know how to recognize the hand of the Almighty in those events that occur sporadically— when the powerful are dethroned and the lowly are exalted, when the rich are sent away empty-handed and the needy are filled. Today the world insistently calls for recognition of man's full dignity and for social equality among all classes. Christians and all men of good will cannot but go along with this demand, even if it means that they must give up their privileges and their personal fortunes for more equitable distribution in the social community.

"Letter to Peoples of the Third World," signed by 18 Third World Catholic Bishops, in Between Honesty and Hope, p. 6

however, that these two general categories—of society's outsiders and rejects on one hand, and of society's acceptable people and systems on the other hand—provided for Jesus and the early church a general rule as to the identification of friendly and enemy territory. What's more, these beliefs of Jesus were not just theoretical; his actions and experiences confirmed his judgment of who his friends and enemies were.

In this regard today, things have become quite different. In fact, the tables have been almost totally turned. The assumption of the Christian churches in the western nations has over the centuries evolved in such a way that there is now an almost opposite identification of friendly and enemy worlds. Not just "obedience where possible," but a firm alliance exists between church and state. Christians are taught by the churches to give the state honor, trust, loyalty and respect. There is seldom even a hint of the old belief that worldly government is under the influence of principalities and powers of darkness. In many cases, Christianity is even the state church; and where it is not the state church, it is most certainly in the position of being the state's chaplain. The Christian religion is now seen as authenticator of the values and morality of society as a whole. Christianity has now become our civil religion.

Ironically, this alliance between church and state has proven most effective in carrying out cooperative efforts to *rescue* people from the very territory which Jesus once found friendly, but is now considered to be enemy territory: the world of the lowly and powerless, the world of society's outcasts and oppressed. Where once the enemy was whatever forces in society create the conditions of the outcast, now the enemy has become the outcasts themselves.

The very people among whom the Gospel was born and from whom the church first sprang, somehow became identified as the ones to whom missionaries must go in order to rescue them from the enemy. This turnabout in the definition of friends and enemies has had a powerful influence in the understanding of the task of Christian mission. The vast majority of Christians in mainline western denominations are white and middle class people whose loyalty to the rulers of this age is often on a par with, or supersedes their loyalty to God. An understanding of

Have your beliefs about a Christian's relation to the state altered since World War II? Since the war in Vietnam? Since Watergate?

Do your beliefs encourage or discourage criticism of our government, and its policies with regard to the arms race, nuclear weapons, civil rights, etc?

Some people refer to the "cooperative task" in our society, of the church, the schools and the police. Does this cooperation make good citizens? Does it make good Christians?

Does the "doctrine of separation of church and state," as you understand it, keep the church and state apart, or does it help maintain a friendly alliance?

Escaping from the world is one extreme. In the other direction are those who use God as an instrument for riches. An example is the brochure from which the following quotes are taken. Its title is: *"IT IS GOD'S WILL THAT YOU PROSPER"*

When you look around you, do others seem to have the best and most of everything that you would like to have? You've noticed their fine cars, furniture, good clothes, nice homes, high paying jobs . . . well, *why can't you have them also,* as God has promised to give all that love Him SUCCESS and GOOD FORTUNE! "Beloved, I wish above all things that you prosper and be in good health!" (3 John 2)

Just return this Post Card to me. Then I will send you "God's Health, Happiness and Prosperity Plan" to start financial blessings flowing toward your life. It will be yours to prove that God will bless and help you. After you receive this package, put it with your bills; the gas bill, the telephone bill, the light bill and other bills which you may have. This plan will help you to *PUT GOD FIRST* in your life so that He might *PUT YOU FIRST!*

Yours for greater success
Rev. Al

"No one can serve two masters; for either he will hate the one and love the other, or he will be devoted to the one and despise the other. You cannot serve God and mammon. . . ."

Matthew 6:24

the world as seen from the point of view of the "broken majority" is almost never given serious consideration.

As strong as these assumptions have become among us, however, they no longer represent an uncontested point of view. Particularly among Third World Christians, this identification of "friends" and "enemies" is being strongly challenged. Those who have themselves been "rescued" are raising the question as to whether they have been used more than they have been helped, and whether they have been taken advantage of more than they have been given advantages. Wherever struggles against systemic injustice are taking place, Christians who are involved in those struggles are confronting traditional assumptions about "friends" and "enemies" of the Faith. They are calling for a re-examination of the soil in which the church is planted, and in which its roots are given food and strength.

The Roots of the Church: Among the Broken Ones of the World

The church was born, has its roots and still finds its life, message and mission among the broken ones of the world. Jesus was born, lived and died identifying with the poor and oppressed. He himself was one of them. The message of liberation and the mission of bringing it to reality is rooted among those whom the world rejects.

This basic fact about Christianity makes a great difference in understanding what it means to join God in mission in the world. If these friends of Jesus—the broken ones—are no longer the soil in which the church has its roots, everything changes. If instead the church tries to root itself among the successful and powerful of the world, the result is a distorted sense of triumphalism, a denial of the cross and a mission of welfare pity and charity towards those whom Jesus loved most and with whom he was himself identified.

For example, when discussion of the mission of the church takes place, and the question of "social ministry" arises (it's usually a side question; almost never in the middle where it should be), it is important to listen carefully to the language we

Hear this, you who trample upon the needy,
   and bring the poor of the land to an end
saying, "When will the new moon be over,
   that we may sell grain?
And the sabbath,
   that we may offer wheat for sale,
that we may make the ephah small and
   the shekel great,
   and deal deceitfully with false balances,
that we may buy the poor for
   silver and the needy
for a pair of sandals,
   and sell the refuse of the wheat?"
The Lord has sworn by the pride of Jacob:
   "Surely I will never forget any of their deeds. . . ."
                         Amos 8:4-7

Who are the "broken ones" today, in whom and with whom
the Church of Jesus Christ has its primary roots? Do you identify
yourself as one of them and in solidarity with them? Can you add
to the following list of "broken ones?"

the sick	lonely
imprisoned	alcoholic
aged	prostitute
dying	divorced
poor	handicapped
welfare	orphans

Do you agree that these are the majority of the world, and that
the western churches are generally disassociated from them?

use. When we ask such typical questions as "What should be the church's response to the poor and oppressed?", we will be revealing a belief that "the church" is something quite separate from "the poor and oppressed"; they are two different things responding to each other, rather than one and the same thing. When the church is not seen as rooted in and identified with the broken ones, then the poor and oppressed are clearly outsiders, and the only response to the question "what should be the church's response to the poor and oppressed?", will of course be condescending, paternalistic charity.

However, if the church is consciously identified with the poor and oppressed rather than thinking of them as separate identities outside the church, the question would be stated differently; the church would then raise the question, "What should be the response of the *rich* to the poor and oppressed?" And since the whole church, and not just a rich segment of the people, would be raising the question, it would be possible to answer the question in terms of justice rather than in terms of charity.

This same example could be applied not only to the poor and oppressed, but to every form of human brokenness, including our own. In fact, it is only through our personal identification as broken ones—sick, dying and in need of the healing touch of wholeness—that the Gospel of Jesus Christ can make sense to us. Only as we identify with (and our own selves as) the broken ones of the world, can the Christian faith make sense. But this cannot be, so long as the broken ones are "objects" outside the church, who are targets of the church's mission. Such persons are "subjects" who are closest to the heart of Jesus, and find themselves at the very base of the church.

That which is most easily lost to us in the western church, because of our identification with the rich and powerful and successful, is the fact that the Gospel is rooted in, and most clearly defined by those who are identified with the broken ones of the world. It is no wonder that it comes to us as such a surprise that the theme of "justice" is not at the edge of the Gospel's concern, but at its center. It comes as an even greater surprise, then, to discover that Christians who join God in mission are called upon to risk their lives in struggles for justice.

The Gospels usually picture the "whole, the rich, the successful" learning the good news from the broken ones. And the good news is that they are not "whole" as they think, and that they are broken with all the rest, and that they can be made whole again by identifying with the broken ones. For example: Jesus then said to the Jews who had believed in him, "If you continue in my word, you are truly my disciples, and you will know the truth, and the truth will make you free." They answered him, "We are descendants of Abraham, and have never been in bondage to any one. How is it that you say, 'You will be made free'?"

Jesus answered them, "Truly, truly, I say to you, every one who commits sin is a slave to sin. The slave does not continue in the house for ever; the son continues for ever. So if the Son makes you free, you will be free indeed."

Or, to put it another way:

This, then, is the great humanistic and historical task of the oppressed: to liberate themselves and their oppressors as well. The oppressors, who oppress, exploit, and rape by virtue of their power, cannot find in this power the strength to liberate either the oppressed or themselves. Only power that springs from the weakness of the oppressed will be sufficiently strong to free both. Any attempt to "soften" the power of the oppressor in deference to the weakness of the oppressed almost always manifests itself in the form of false generosity; indeed the attempt never goes beyond this. In order to have the continued opportunity to express their "generosity," the oppressors must perpetuate injustice as well. An unjust social order is the permanent fount of this "generosity," which is nourished by death, despair, and poverty. That is why the dispensers of false generosity become desperate at the slightest threat to its source.

True generosity consists precisely in fighting to destroy the causes which nourish false charity. False charity constrains the fearful and subdued, the "rejects of life," to extend their trembling hands. True generosity lies in striving so that these hands—whether of individuals or entire peoples—need be extended less and less in supplication, so that more and more they become human hands which work and, working, transform the world.

p. 28, 29, Paulo Freire, *Pedogogy Of The Oppressed*, Seabury, 1973

B. MISSION IS STRUGGLE

Joining God in mission in the world means to participate in a deadly struggle. The Scriptures leave little to the imagination in describing this reality in violent military language. There is a battle being waged on enemy territory. It is a war between God and Satan. Satan assumes many forms, although his favorite one seems to be that of the authorities and rulers of each age.

The prize being fought over is the entire creation, including ourselves. The ultimate outcome of the battle is already assured. The lamb who was slain has begun his reign. However the fate of each one of us is still being determined.

As each one of us is rescued (liberated) from the enemy's concentration camps, our arrival and our new life in freedom is joyously celebrated. Then each of us is ourselves prepared to join the battle. We are trained and equipped to join God in the continuing struggle against the enemy.

For the early Christians, who were society's outcasts to begin with, and who became even more so because of their identification with their new faith, the "struggle" was not just a spiritual one. It involved their whole being, and involved their continued facing of imprisonment, torture, and death at the hands of governmental authorities. For the majority of people today the mission of the church is likewise not just a spiritual struggle. Rather it involves the confronting of brokenness and oppression of the whole person and of the whole community. The reality of the world, as described in the first section of this study, is the reality of brokenness and struggle for wholeness within which the mission of the church takes place.

Yet, over the centuries, as the church identified more and more with the successful and the powerful, the idea of "struggle" has increasingly been discounted and underplayed. In the following pages, three important issues are discussed. Each of them—dualism, individualism and triumphalism—comes in direct conflict with the understanding that the mission of Christians is to participate with the broken ones of the world in the struggle for wholeness. Each of these three are serious

110

Following are excerpts from an address entitled "In Christ-One Community In The Spirit," by Bishop Manas Buthelezi of the Evangelical Lutheran Church In Southern Africa. The address was delivered at the 1977 Assembly of the Lutheran World Federation in Dar Es Salaam, and was instrumental in having that assembly officially recognize that the situation of South African apartheid requires "public and unequivocal" rejection by Christians.

The classical distinction between the church militant and the church triumphant carries a significance for our time that lies beyond merely understanding these phrases as references to the church on earth and the church in heaven. When oppressed groups of people all over the world are engaged in one form of struggle for liberation or another, it may be illuminating to speak of *a living church—as a struggling church*. By struggle here is meant an active commitment to the pursuance of means for the attainment of an objective that enhances the well-being of the people of God as an expression of service to God. To speak of the church militant is to speak of a church committed to a cause of struggle . . .

The victorious Christ is thus only the obverse side of a struggling or *a fighting Christ*. On earth the church spearheads the cosmic movement for continuing and accomplishing that which Christ initiated. In and through the church the struggle of Christ continues. The church shares with Christ in continuing the struggle for a cosmos that awaits liberation, "because the creation itself will be set free from its bondage to decay and obtain the glorious liberty of the children of God. We know that the whole creation has been groaning in travail together until now." (Romans 8:21-22)

The struggle of the church, like that of Christ, is not against man, but for man. To the glory of God it seeks to further whatever promotes the well-being of man and to destroy whatever oppresses man and keeps him in bondage.

111

problems which especially plague the mission of the church in the United States.

The Struggle For Justice vs. Dualism

Our attention has already been directed several times to the issue of dualism, with its dichotomy of body and soul, world and spirit. There are few problems more serious than dualism's ability to confuse and distract from the real issues. When the task of evangelism and conversion is defined simply as a "spiritual" task, and other "worldly" concerns are given lesser significance, a conflict is created that was never created in the ministry of Jesus.

The conflict that is created by dualism is that the issue of injustice is removed from the center of Christian concern. The effects of political/economic oppression are measured in terms which suggest that systemic damage to the mind and body of a person is separable from, and less serious than its effect on the soul. Biblical and theological scholarship is recognizing more and more that the Gospel addresses itself to the "whole person." The battle between God and Satan that is taking place at this moment, and in which we participate, is not a battle for a segment of the human personality called the "soul", but is a total battle for the complete and indivisible person created in God's own image.

The problem of dualism is not only theological, but also political. The question that must be asked is who it is that benefits when dualism reigns victorious, and the issues of justice for the minds and bodies of people are ignored? As long as attention is paid exclusively to the souls of oppressed peoples, there is no threat to the systems which benefit from their oppression. When oppressed peoples are taught that the Exodus story or the message of Jesus are intended only for the benefit of the salvation of their eternal souls, they know who it is that benefits from such teachings. And it isn't hard to figure out who it is that pays for their evangelization! Participation with God in mission in the world is a mandate to struggle for justice and to work against the oppression caused by dualism.

Finally, be strong in the Lord and in the strength of his might. Put on the whole armor of God, that you may be able to stand against the wiles of the devil. For we are not contending against flesh and blood, but against the principalities, against the powers, against the world rulers of this present darkness, against the spiritual hosts of wickedness in the heavenly places. Therefore take the whole armor of God, that you may be able to withstand in the evil day, and having done all, to stand. Stand therefore, having girded your loins with truth, and having put on the breastplate of righteousness, and having shod your feet with the equipment of the gospel of peace; above all taking the shield of faith, with which you can quench all the flaming darts of the evil one. And take the helmet of salvation, and the sword of the Spirit, which is the word of God.

We Christians . . . are ourselves responsible for the misuse of the resources God has given to the world. And our responsibility is not merely as persons for other people, but also for the political and economic structures that bring about poverty, injustice and violence. Today our responsibility has a new dimension because men now have the power to remove the causes of the evil, whose symptoms alone they could treat before.

> Report of the Beirut Conference on World Development, sponsored by the World Council of Churches and the Pontifical Commission on Justice and Peace, p. 15

Capitalism has set up once more the idols execrated of old by the people of God—mannon, Baal and Astharte. Filipino Christians have the obligation to smash these idols enshrined in the capitalist structure, both in its foreign neocolonial aspect and in its domestic semi-feudal manifestations. We must set up new alternative political and economic structures that will promote the full human development of our people. We must collaborate in building a new world order wherein men will strive not for selfish gain but for service to the common good of the human race.

> Statement of the Christian Filipino Democratic Movement, July 1971, in IDOC-NA, no. 33, p. 26.

Corporate Struggle vs. Individualism

The task of struggling for justice for the "whole person" is important, but it is also incomplete. No one can be a whole person by themselves. A whole person must also be a part of a whole community. Another kind of deadly divisiveness takes place when the individual and community are separated from each other. In North America, the idolatry of individualism and the cult of personality have become our normal and celebrated way of life. Christianity is often identified as an individualistic brand of religion that places primary emphasis on one's own personal salvation and a vertical relation with God. Wherever Christian mission is based on the promulgation of this kind of community-less religion, something quite different from the Holy Catholic Church, the Communion of Saints is the result.

Biblically based Christianity, if it is nothing else, is God addressing us as a corporate people, as a community. The result of sin is the destruction of community—the alienation of individuals from God and from each other. God's redemptive mission is the reconciliation of creation and the restoration of community. The church is a special community of God—the Communion of Saints—who celebrate this restoration to community and who are called to a collective task. Community and corporateness are essential and central to the Christian faith. There can be no whole persons outside the whole community.

However, this "community" to which we are referring is not only the Christian community. The "ship of the church" which is sailing through the ocean of the world is not a private cruising vessel without contact with others. Rather, it regularly docks at every port of call in the world. Our mission with God is to address the root causes of brokenness in the corporate life of all people in the world: in families, tribes, cities, nations, cultures, political/economic systems, etc. As Christians commit themselves to ministry among persons who suffer from sickness, poverty and despair, we must also join with such persons in the struggle against the systemic and corporate causes of their problems, as well as the search for systemic and corporate solutions.

From the point of view of the poor, the oppressed and others who are unable to disguise their brokenness, this dualism not only divides the physical world from the spiritual world; more importantly, it creates a two-sided world of upper and lower classes. Still more tragic: the Christian churches have historically identified with the upper classes. For example, read the following passage by Orlando Carvajal of the Philippines:

Many values, attitudes, orientations, and biases that are often presumed to be part of a distinctively Christian outlook simply stem from the conditions of material life of a particular social class in a dualist society. Christians, historically, first belong to a particular class with all its attending material conditions. This class position determines their basic outlook on reality. This class position forms the basic framework within which they interpret their faith and integrate it with reality. Thus, the dualist worldview of Christians belonging to the ruling class provides them with the categories to interpret religion, dogma, and the Bible in a manner that justifies the present social order and perpetuates their privileged position in that order. Since the institutional church is part of the propertied ruling class, it protects its vested interests against the challenge hurled at the system by Christians of the working class. All this is done in the name of upholding sound Christian doctrine. On the other hand, the dynamic outlook of Christians belonging to the working class is radicalizing their approach to Christianity, and not vice-versa.

Orlando Carvajal
"Doing Theological Reflection In
a Philippine Context," p. 111
The Emergent Gospel
Torres and Fabella, Ed.
Orbis, 1978

Above all, the persistent dichotomy between "mission to individuals" and "mission to society" must be done away with. This false and unnatural division has been a plague to the church far too long. The debate between those who believe that "changing individuals is the way to change the systems" and those who believe that "changing systems is the way to change individuals," is an unproductive debate that is doomed from the start because it is based on such a false dichotomy.

Another equally false, but very popular myth is that a ministry of "one on one" is a way of dealing with injustice. It is based on a circular kind of logic which says that the system can be changed by caring for the individuals that the system destroys.

The question of whether individuals or systems must first be changed cannot be answered because it is a false question based on a false view of the world and of the Christian faith. There can be no concept of mission that permits a dichotomy—neither in concept nor in programs—between mission to individuals and mission which emphasizes the building of community and participation in struggles for political/economic systems that are just and human.

Theology of the Cross vs. Triumphalism

A subject which we have already approached in various parts of this study, although not specifically identified by name, is that of "Triumphalism." This is a disease, apparently easily contracted by Christians, which is evidenced by expectations that the church on earth will be powerful and successful, rather than being found among those who are suffering and struggling, broken and rejected. Triumphalism is the attempt to substitute the "church triumphant" (a name used to describe the church in the Kingdom of Heaven) for the "church militant" (a name used to describe the church struggling to join God in mission in the world). Triumphalism is based on a "theology of glory"; the church militant is based on a "theology of the cross." Triumphalism identifies with power, success and the rulers of this world. The theology of the cross identifies with the suffering of broken people and their struggle for wholeness.

116

Read this statement from an interview with a Christian in China today. Do his words help us to deal with our exaggerated individualism?

(Shao was asked at this point if Christians in China would say that God was revealing Himself in the Chinese Revolution. To this he answered, "I consider the moral ideal of 'serving the people' is over all.")

Our task (in the Institute on World Religions) is to present the significance of religion in human history within the Chinese academic community. Understanding between our two peoples will not happen overnight. There is a language barrier, and our value systems differ. Words have vastly different meanings. "Liberalism" has a bad sound in Chinese. "Individualism" is seen as "selfishness." Human rights can't be seen in a vacuum, but within historical contexts. Christian mission today is to develop understanding between our people.

"A Chinese Visitor in America," an interview with Shao Fusan, an Episcopal Priest in China, from Doc No. 4.1.2.36, LWF Marxism and China Study, Information Letter #25, p. 19.

Even those things which are normally an individual's choice can become a matter for the Christian community to speak with a totally unified voice, and a matter of obligatory obedience to Christ. For example, when an evil and racist regime such as that which rules in South Africa defines good as evil and evil as good, and bases its definitions on what is purported to be the word of God, then the whole church must speak out and call all its individual members to obligatory resistance.

The Christian Crusades in the Middle Ages, and the Holy Roman Empire are only two examples of the triumphalism that fills the pages of history of the Christian Church. More recent illustrations can be found wherever the church is allied with particular political or economic systems, or when the churches are identified exclusively with privileged races and classes of people.

Popular beliefs about missionaries among western Christians are still today heavily influenced by the triumphalism that crept into the missionary movement of the last two centuries. It is no accident that the colonial politics of the western nations and the twisted ideas about "Christianizing savages" developed at the same time. There are few more important tasks among Christians today than to separate the mission of the church from triumphalistic colonial concepts that are associated with bringing western "civilization" and development to the rest of the world.

The alternative to triumphalistic Christianity is the identification of ourselves and our mission with the broken ones of the world. Joining God in mission is to follow Jesus in his becoming one among those whom society pushes to its edges. The "theology of the cross" understands Jesus as calling us to faithfulness by offering us a cross and a command to pick up the cross and follow him. Jesus calls us to participate in such struggles against all the forces of injustice and oppression in the world, as an expression of our faith that in him and his cross and resurrection all brokenness in the world and in our lives is overcome.

C. THE GLOBAL/LOCAL FOCUS OF MISSION

The development of the overseas missionary movement more than two centuries ago marked the beginning of a global consciousness that is still undergoing development; it is being radically revised even at this present moment. This global awareness has confirmed and expanded the Biblical understanding of the universality and interconnectedness of the Body of Christ. The presence of the church in every land and nation is

Read the following action taken by the Lutheran World Federation, meeting in Dar Es Salaam in 1977. Do you agree with its conclusion?

"Under normal circumstances, Christians may have different opinions in political questions. However, political and social systems might become perverted and oppressive so that it is consistent with the (Augsburg) confession to reject them and to work for change. We especially appeal to our white member churches in southern Africa to recognize that the situation in southern Africa constitutes a *status confessionis*. This means that, on the basis of faith and in order to manifest the unity of the church, churches would publicly and unequivocally reject the existing apartheid system."

—Sixth Assembly of the Lutheran World Federation, 1977

Page through the hymnal of your church. Compare the hymns that are written with the personal pronouns I and me, with those hymns based on the collective pronouns of we and us. Do they give different messages? Which do you find the most appealing?

a proclamation of the oneness of the human family and of the sisterhood and brotherhood of all humankind.

Along with the vast international changes that have been taking place politically and economically in recent decades, a comparable change is taking place in the understanding of global Christian mission. These changes correspond to our description of global realities in the first part of this study. The mission of the church is decreasingly being described in terms of geographical movement of missionaries and resources from one part of the world to another. Rather it is being recognized that the very same issues and tasks permeate all areas of the world in interlocking and interrelated ways. Both the causes and solutions to problems in every part of the world are interdependent.

Christ's missionary mandate still urgently calls us into the world. But the call is not from one place of strength to another place of weakness; the call is not from one place with ready answers to another place with searching questions; the call is not from a civilized part of the world into farflung distant lands of savage ignorance and idolatry. In every place and nation, *including our own*, one can find the terror and violence-filled problems of savage ignorance and idolatry, of brokenness and oppression.

In our situation, however, it is a far more difficult set of conditions because the problems are covered up with a thin facade of "civilization" and "progress." The call to mission is a call for us to go deeply into the world of our own reality, into the savageness and brutality, the idolatry and ignorance of our own situation. The call, in every place and nation, *including our own*, is to join the struggle for justice and rightness, and to join the efforts to build communities of faithful and celebrating servants of God. And our call is to do this with a consciousness of solidarity with sisters and brothers carrying out the same mission in all parts of the world.

This new perspective in the global/local interrelationship of mission has a double effect on us. On the one hand it changes the way United States Christians relate to peoples and churches in the rest of the world. We are being required to seriously revise the distorted sense of self importance we western people have

On these final pages are printed a few litanies, prayers, and hymns which you may wish to use. All of them are songs of hope, and prayers for the future, expressing confidence that our brokenness and the brokenness of the world can be given the gift of wholeness through its creating, liberating, providing and limiting God.

L: Thus says the Lord, the Almighty God: "Behold, I am doing a new thing: now it springs forth, do you not perceive it?"

P: Your new thing, Lord, is the beginning of our revolutions.

L: Thus says the Lord, the King of Israel and his Redeemer, the Lord of Hosts: "I am the first and I am the last; besides me there is no God."

P: There is no corporate power, no economic system, there is no military authority, nor defense establishment that we want to serve besides you. Save us from our idols. Save us from our overwhelming needs for security. Your Lordship frees us to live without fear of oppression, without need for exploitative relationships. Help us to be free to risk.

L: "Who has announced from of old the things to come? Let them tell us what is yet to be."

P: Your word, O God, is the source of our ongoing life together. In it we discover new directions and resurrected life. We struggle not to forget your mighty deeds of old, nor the people like us, all the saints, who struggled to be faithful. We struggle to live up to our responsibilities now, to live lives reflecting your love and justice. We don't want to leave our children the present structures of hate and inhumanity. The future also belongs to you.

L: "Fear not, nor be afraid: have I not told you from of old and declared it? And you are my witnesses!"

P: Yes, Lord, witnesses to your greatest New Thing, the Resurrected One, Jesus Christ, who conquered all the powers of death and hell, who frees us from our bondages and sin, who empowers us even now to wrestle with principalities and powers that hinder the renewal of all creation.

> Litany by participants in a conference on "The Church And The Revolution," in St. Louis, November 1979

tended to give ourselves in relation to the rest of the world. Especially the exposure of the role of western nations in maintaining conditions of injustice and oppression, combined with the growing strength and wisdom of those churches throughout the Third World which we once euphemistically called "daughters," ought to have something of a humbling effect on us. And it ought to be creating new dynamics in our international church relationships.

On the other hand, and perhaps even more importantly for the purpose of a concluding statement for this study of mission—this new global awareness also dramatically changes the way we look at ourselves and the way we do mission in our own home settings. Our own values and lifestyles, our own political and economic systems, as well as our understanding of the mission of the church locally, all take on new meaning when seen from within a larger global context.

Is it possible for us to think of a giant international spotlight illuminating our own backyards, our neighborhoods and our local churches? Can we conceive of representatives from churches of the Third World visiting us and helping us to evaluate and redefine the mission of the church in the place where we live?

Twenty centuries ago, St. Paul received a call from Macedonia to bring the Gospel to a new place. This "Macedonian Call" has been a symbol for missionary work ever since. If a "Macedonian Call" is still being given today, it is we who should be issuing the call to the churches of the Third World to "come on over" and help us to understand the meaning of the Gospel for our day. For centuries we have been received as missionaries and "bearers of the Gospel" by peoples throughout the world. Now this procedure must begin to be reversed. The call must go out for bearers of the Gospel to come to us. The experiences of the Third World peoples have prepared them in special ways for the future, and have given them an understanding of the task of Christians in our day. We need to listen, to learn, to receive the gift of their knowledge and experience.

In a limited way, this study of the Bible and mission has been an effort to have this experience begin to take place. A majority

A Shorter Catechism of Hope

L: What is hope?
R: Hope is a mother awaiting the birth of her child . . .
R: a band of Blacks singing: "We are climbing Jacob's ladder". . .
R: a young woman on her wedding day . . .
R: a little child looking forward to Christmas . . .
R: a fanfare of drums announcing an African eucharist . . .
R: an oppressed person returning good for evil . . .
R: a choir of lepers singing the Hallelujah Chorus . . .
R: Jesus praying for his enemies . . .
   A moment of silence

L: When does hope appear?
R: when I walk through the valley of the shadow of death . . .
R: when I hear Bortniansky's "Hymn to the Cherubim" . . .
R: when another person becomes Christ for me . . .
R: when a sick child smiles through his pain . . .
R: when God mocks the power of nations . . .
R: when the congregation says Kyrie Eleison, and means what it says . . .
R: when I see non-Christians practicing the Sermon on the Mount . . .
R: when I obey Christ's command to pray for my enemies . . .
   A moment of silence
L: What are the signs that this hope is the Lord's doing?
R: the miraculous healing of animosities . . .
R: the surprising forgiveness by another, when I could not forgive myself . . .
R: the mysterious release of joy in the midst of tears . . .
R: the unexpected upsurge of freedom and energy . . .
R: the strengthening of bonds to all God's people . . .
R: the assurance of the Spirit moving in my heart . . .
   A moment of silence

Continued on page 125.

123

of the quotes and references in the right hand columns have come from persons and churches in the Third World. In nearly all these references, U.S. Christians are called to a new sense of mission in our own country and our own local setting.

From this larger, international contest, we are urged to hear Christ's call to repentance, conversion and new life. We are called away from our triumphalistic identification with the powerful and to a new identification with the broken ones of the world. We are called to a new awareness of our own brokenness.

We are called to the realization that there is no way into a justly-shared world without our giving up our unjust share of the world. There is no way to achieve the empowerment of the powerless without losing our power to control, dominate and consume the rest of the world.

We have a mission to our own people; it is not our mission alone, but a joining of God's mission in isolation from the church's mission in the rest of the world. Instead, it is a mission at home which needs to be brought into harmony with the mission of the church globally. If we work at doing this, we will be achieving far more than any program of foreign missions.

Our mission to our own people is to bring our broken reality into the illuminating light of the international and universal healing Gospel of Jesus Christ. Under this light we can become incorporated into God's mission, which is to bring us and the whole world beyond our brokenness into wholeness.

L: Why does God give this gift?
R: to free us from fear and anxiety . . .
R: to enable us to share the sufferings of our neighbors . . .
R: to give us power to proclaim the joys of salvation . . .
R: to welcome friends and enemies into the fellowship of the forgiven . . .
R: to impel us to glorify God for his goodness to all . . .
A moment of silence
The Gloria in Excelsis, said or sung

Giving Account Of The Hope
World Council of Churches, 1975

O Healing River, send down your water.
Send down your water upon this land.
O healing river send down your water,
And wash the blood from off the sand.
The land is parching, the land is thirsting
No seed is growing on this barren ground.
O healing river send down your water.
O healing river, send your water down.

O seed of freedom, awake and flourish.
Let deep roots nourish, let the talk stalk rise.
O healing river send down your water.
O healing river send your waters down.

O seed of freedom, Burst forth in glory.
Proud leaves unfurling into the skies.
O healing river send down your water
O healing river, send your waters down.